LIN-MANUEL MIRANDA

RAISING THEATER TO NEW HEIGHTS

D0067849

TRAILBLAZERS

Neil Armstrong

Jackie Robinson

Harriet Tubman

Jane Goodall

Albert Einstein

Beyoncé

Stephen Hawking

Simone Biles

Martin Luther King Jr.

J. K. Rowling

Amelia Earhart

Lin-Manuel Miranda

LIN-MANUEL MIRANDA
RAISING THEATER TO NEW HEIGHTS

KURTIS SCALETTA

RANDOM HOUSE  NEW YORK

All rights reserved. Published in the United States by Random House Children's Books,
a division of Penguin Random House LLC, New York.

Random House and the colophon are registered trademarks of Penguin Random House LLC.

Visit us on the Web! rhcbooks.com

Educators and librarians, for a variety of teaching tools, visit us at
RHTeachersLibrarians.com

Library of Congress Cataloging-in-Publication Data is available upon request.
ISBN 978-0-593-12446-8 (trade pbk.)
ISBN 978-0-593-12447-5 (lib. bdg.)
ISBN 978-0-593-12448-2 (ebook)

Created by Stripes Publishing Limited, an imprint of the Little Tiger Group

Printed in the United States of America

10 9 8 7 6 5 4 3 2 1

First Edition

Random House Children's Books supports the First Amendment
and celebrates the right to read.

Contents

INTRODUCTION

AM NOT THROWING AWAY MY SHOT

On May 12, 2009, Lin-Manuel Miranda decided to *not* do what the president had asked. The White House had invited the twenty-nine-year-old singer and composer to perform in an evening of poetry, music, and the spoken word. The event was a showcase of diversity in the arts, especially "voices that are often not heard." Guests included poet Joshua Bennett, actor James Earl Jones, and musician Esperanza Spalding. The audience was a mix of politicians, reporters, and college students from the Washington, DC, area, including President Barack Obama and his wife, Michelle. The event was streamed live on the official White House website.

Lin-Manuel was expected to sing a song from *In the Heights*, his award-winning musical about Latino people living in New York City. It was a perfect fit for the evening, but Lin-Manuel had a better idea. Instead, he told the audience he was going to perform a song about a historical figure who "embodied hip-hop":

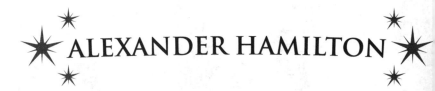

ALEXANDER HAMILTON

The audience laughed. Alexander Hamilton? The guy
on the ten-dollar bill? What did Alexander Hamilton,
who lived more than 250 years ago, have to do with
hip-hop?

Lin-Manuel was taking a big chance. He had no idea
what the audience would think. Only two people besides
him had heard the song. One was Lin-Manuel's fiancée,
Vanessa. The other was Alex Lacamoire, who played
piano that night. Maybe everybody else would hate it.

He sang the song anyway. The worst thing that could happen, he figured, was that he would find out the song wasn't as good as he thought. He launched into what would go on to become the opening song of the musical *Hamilton*, which tells the story of an immigrant who rose from obscurity and poverty. His energetic performance and clever rhymes won over the room. Suddenly, this forgotten American hero felt important and modern. Hamilton's ambition, rivalries, scandals, and deft wordplay made sense with the hip-hop music. Everyone in the audience knew they were seeing something special. Michelle Obama snapped her fingers in time to the beat, and President Obama was the first to jump to his feet in applause when Lin-Manuel finished.

The whole day was a day that will exist outside any other day in my life.

A popular comedian made fun of the bit the next day, but being spoofed on TV didn't bother Lin-Manuel. He'd seen the audience's astonished smiles and heard their applause. At the time, Lin-Manuel had written only one song, but he had plans for writing more about the American forefather. Originally, he wanted to compose enough material for an album, which he was calling *The Hamilton Mixtape*, but now he thought he could take it even further. Maybe he could pursue the crazy dream that had been tempting him: to write an entire show about Alexander Hamilton.

This quintessentially American story, a rags-to-riches tale about an immigrant who succeeded on the strength of his writing and hard work, had swept Lin-Manuel away, and he was ready to bring it to the masses.

$\gtrless$ SMASH HIT $\lessgtr$

Six years later, on January 20, 2015, *Hamilton: An American Musical* opened for previews at the off-Broadway Public Theater in New York.

Musicals are expensive and time-consuming productions to stage. There are millions of dollars invested in even a small show, and four to five years of work for the writers. Sometimes a group of writers, performers, and investors spend all that time and money just to see their show close after a bad first week. Every major production is a risk, but *Hamilton* was a bigger risk than most for several reasons.

The first was its subject. Tickets to Broadway shows are expensive, with even the cheapest tickets priced at close to a hundred dollars, so audiences tend to pick familiar stories or songs. For many years, Broadway had relied on reprises of classics, reboots of popular movies, and "jukebox musicals" crafted around well-known songs. For example, two of the biggest shows the summer *Hamilton* debuted were based on the classic

Disney movies *The Lion King* and *Aladdin*. A third, *Mamma Mia!*, was built around the hit songs of the European pop band ABBA. With new music and a story about a lesser-known historical figure, *Hamilton* was definitely a gamble for audiences. Though an important figure in American history, this founding father was not as well-known as his friends and rivals George Washington and Thomas Jefferson.

Another reason *Hamilton* was a risk was its musical style. Hip-hop hadn't really been a style used in musicals. The two Broadway musicals that had featured hip-hop, *Bring It On* and *In the Heights*, were previous projects by Lin-Manuel Miranda. A third, *Venice*, had run at the same off-Broadway theater but never made it to Broadway. Most worrying, *Holler If Ya Hear Me*, a jukebox musical featuring the songs of rapper Tupac Shakur, had been one of Broadway's biggest flops in recent memory, closing after just a month. The usual audiences of Broadway shows were not fans of hip-hop, and the people who loved hip-hop didn't go to musicals. They were two different worlds.

Where Exactly IS Broadway?

Broadway is a street in Manhattan, New York, that runs through the Theater District. However, the term "Broadway" usually refers to a theater's size, not its address. Theaters with 500 or more seats are considered "Broadway"; theaters with 100 to 499 seats are "off-Broadway"; and those that have fewer than 100 seats are "off-off-Broadway." There are 41 official Broadway theaters in the Theater District.

Many shows start off-Broadway, giving the cast and directors a chance to perfect the show before they are open to a wider audience

The off-Broadway Public Theater—where *Hamilton* previewed—is actually a bit closer to Broadway, the street, than the on-Broadway Richard Rodgers Theatre, where it made its "Broadway" debut.

OFF-BROADWAY   **BROADWAY**

Perhaps the biggest risk of staging *Hamilton* was that the original cast was almost entirely made up of people of color, with no major stars. Lin-Manuel Miranda, Christopher Jackson, and Renée Elise Goldsberry, who played Hamilton, George Washington, and Angelica Schuyler, respectively, were familiar to Broadway fans but were hardly known to tourists, who make up a large share of ticket sales.

But the combination of these three factors was what made *Hamilton* and Lin-Manuel's creative vision truly original. Black, Asian, and Latino actors playing America's founders and rapping their dialogue was something that would surprise many people, but it worked. The music was catchy, the lyrics smart and funny, and the actors and singers energetic.

Based on word of mouth, *Hamilton*'s planned one-month run at the Public Theater was sold out by opening night. Everybody was talking about this new show, and everybody

SOLD OUT

wanted to see it. The run was extended, and the cast played to packed houses from January 20 through

SOLD OUT

May 3, 2015.

The buzz could be heard outside of the usual Broadway circles, too. People who didn't go to musicals knew they needed to see *this* one. Even before it opened on Broadway at the Richard Rodgers Theatre in the summer of 2015, over 200,000 tickets had been sold.

Despite the strangeness of historical figures singing modern music, the hip-hop blended so perfectly with the story of political struggles and personal rivalries that the audience never questioned it. The diverse cast humanized historical figures and made them vibrant and relatable. It would not be a good economic decision to mortgage your house to buy tickets, reviews said, but it might be worth it.

"Yes, it really is that good."
—*The New York Times* (August 6, 2015)

Sold-out shows and lines around the block were only the first sign of *Hamilton*'s success. Then the cast recording won a Grammy Award for Best Musical Theater Album, and the play won the Pulitzer Prize for Drama. A beautifully made book with all the lyrics from the musical, photographs from the show, and a behind-the-scenes look at the making of *Hamilton* topped the *New York Times* bestseller list. Overall the show won eleven Tonys, including Best Musical.

Every night there were famous faces in the crowd. Over *Hamilton*'s first year, celebrities as varied as Cher, Paul McCartney, Jay-Z and Beyoncé, the Obamas, tennis star Roger Federer, and Madonna could be spotted in the audience.

And it wasn't just celebrities and critics who raved about *Hamilton*. People across the country streamed the album, getting it to the top of the rap album charts, and planned vacations around a chance to see the show live.

While every year has its new stars and hit shows, few are such sensations across the country, even across the ocean. *Hamilton* was, as *Rolling Stone* magazine declared in an issue with Lin-Manuel on the cover, "the cultural event of our time."

THE MAN BEHIND THE PHENOMENON

Lin-Manuel Miranda, as the creator, quickly became one of the most famous people in the country. Yet he continued to wear his fame as casually as the jeans and T-shirts that made up his daily uniform. He was humble, down-to-earth, committed to his family, and plainly driven by a passion for social justice in both his life and work. Though his youth and energy made people compare him to his subject, Lin-Manuel did not have the bitter rivalries and petty jealousies that marked Hamilton's life. It was clear he wanted to lift everyone else up with him.

CHAPTER 1

HOW FAR I'LL GO

Lin-Manuel Miranda was born in New York City on January 16, 1980. His parents, Luis Miranda and Luz Towns-Miranda, had met in New York, but both were originally from Puerto Rico. Luz's great-great-great-great-grandparents David and Sophie Towns met and married in the 1810s in Virginia. David was white, and Sophia was black. In those days, such relationships were unheard of, and often illegal. The Townses moved to Texas and then to Mexico, trying to find a place where they could raise their family without facing racism and prejudice. Their children and grandchildren spread throughout Texas and Mexico. At least one branch of their family ended up in Puerto Rico, where most of Lin-Manuel's direct family originates.

My mom's side of the family has a history as complicated as our country itself.

Puerto Rico

Puerto Rico is a US territory in the Caribbean. Until Christopher Columbus arrived in 1493, the island of Puerto Rico was inhabited by people called the Taíno, who had spread across the Caribbean. Following the invasion, the island became part of the Spanish Empire and remained so for the next 400 years. Spain eventually lost possession of the island to the US in the Spanish-American War in 1898. Today, most of the 3 million citizens of Puerto Rico have mixed ancestry of European colonizers, formerly enslaved people from Africa, and the native Taíno people.

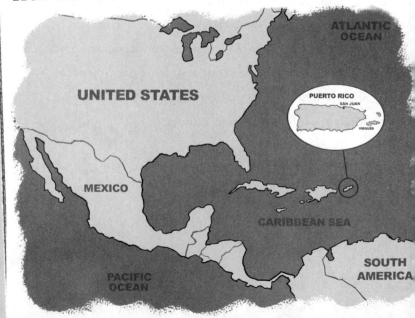

Though Puerto Rico is a US territory, its residents do not have representation in Congress and do not vote for the president of the US. However, Puerto Ricans can move freely between the island and the mainland. Many Puerto Ricans relocated to the mainland in the 20th century because there were more jobs there. Most settled in New York City, especially Manhattan.

Lin-Manuel's father grew up in Vega Alta, Puerto Rico. He was considered to be very clever, and by age seventeen, he was already in college and had a good job managing a department store. But Luis was restless and wanted more. He took the enormous risk of quitting his job and leaving home to move to New York City.

Initially, Luis was interested in becoming a psychiatrist, so he enrolled in a graduate program at New York University. It was there that he met Luz Towns. Luz had also been born in Puerto Rico but had moved to the mainland as a small child with her family. She grew up in New York and New Jersey. The two fell in love and were married less than a year later.

Luz became a clinical psychologist, but Luis ended up going into politics. He spent many years advising New York mayor Ed Koch on issues affecting the Latino population of New York City, among other topics.

Alexander Hamilton and Luis Miranda

Lin-Manuel has said that Alexander Hamilton's story resonated with him, in part because of its similarities to his own father's story:

▸ Both were born in poverty on Caribbean islands.

▸ Both were prodigies who distinguished themselves academically at a young age.

▸ Both moved to New York City when they were about 18 years old to find their fortune.

▸ Both worked in politics.

⋛ EARLY CHILDHOOD ⋚

The newlyweds settled in Inwood, a largely Latino neighborhood at the northern tip of Manhattan, bordering on Washington Heights. In 1973, they had a baby girl, named Luz after her mother. Lin-Manuel followed seven years later.

As a teenager, Luis had saved a clipping of a protest

poem by the Puerto Rican writer José Manuel Torres Santiago. "You are a red baby, Lin-Manuel," the poem's narrator addresses his infant son in Spanish, "and I don't know what you'll be when you grow up." Lin-Manuel got his name from this verse.

Since both Luis and Luz worked full-time in demanding jobs, the Mirandas had a nanny—the same woman who had helped raise Luis in Puerto Rico. Little Luz and Lin-Manuel called her Abuela, or Grandmother, even though she was not related to them. Abuela would greet them after school, make their dinner, and often put them to bed during the week.

On weekends, the family would go for walks to the playground, or to the movies. Sometimes they would go to a Yankees baseball game. They would cheer loudest for Bernie Williams, the longtime Yankee center fielder, who had been born in the same Puerto Rican town as Luis. Lin-Manuel's grandfather had been his Little League coach!

The Mirandas wanted their children to succeed in everything. They raised Luz and Lin-Manuel bilingual, speaking both English and Spanish. And from a young age, they encouraged learning. Lin-Manuel could read books on his own at three years old. At nursery school, he would read to the other children!

⋚ A HOUSE FULL OF MUSIC ⋚

The Miranda house was always full of music, especially soundtracks to films and plays. Family favorites included *Camelot*, *Man of La Mancha*, and *The Unsinkable Molly Brown*. Growing up in a house where show tunes were always on the record player, Lin-Manuel "never had a chance to be anything but a musical theater guy," he has said.

The family also loved Latin music—the music of their roots—and Luis and Luz taught their children how to dance salsa.

Lin-Manuel's favorite musical as a child was a movie—*The Little Mermaid*. He particularly liked Sebastian the crab and his song "Under the Sea." When the song was nominated for an Oscar for Best Original Song in a movie in 1989, Lin-Manuel took interest in the awards show for the first time. As he watched with his family, he promised his mother if *he* ever went to the Oscars, she would be his date on the red carpet.

His feelings about music ran deep. He would burst into tears when listening to certain songs, such as Simon & Garfunkel's "Bridge over Troubled Water" or Stevie Wonder's "I Just Called to Say I Love You." Little Lin-Manuel would try to sing along but would break down with emotion before he reached the chorus. He loved movies with lots of songs but couldn't make it through *Mary Poppins*, either. He'd be too upset by the sadness of "Feed the Birds," a song about a homeless woman, to keep watching.

WINNING THE KINDERGARTEN LOTTERY

At age five, Lin-Manuel qualified for Hunter College Elementary School, a program for gifted children. As a public school, Hunter is free, but it is highly competitive. Students have to pass a difficult test to be considered for a place. For the Mirandas, getting in was like winning the lottery! But for Lin-Manuel, it was nerve-racking. In nursery school, he had felt like an outsider because he was the only child who could read. At Hunter, he felt like an outsider because so many kids were smarter than he was! They read books beyond their years and had deep talks.

This isn't the place for me.

Does Santa really exist?

What's the evidence?

He was scared that he wasn't really cut out for the school, and he worried that he wouldn't fit in. However, Lin-Manuel had a great sense of humor, and he soon discovered that being funny was a good way to get along with anyone and make friends. He quickly gained a reputation as the class clown, the kind of classmate everybody likes—except, at times, the teacher!

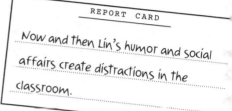

REPORT CARD

Now and then Lin's humor and social affairs create distractions in the classroom.

Hunter College gave Lin-Manuel an environment where he could thrive, but it also isolated him from the Puerto Rican community. There were no other kids from his neighborhood, or any Puerto Rican students at all, in his class. Hunter was in the affluent Upper East Side of Manhattan, and most of his classmates were white and wealthy. When Lin-Manuel visited other Hunter students, he would translate so they could communicate with their Spanish-speaking housekeepers and nannies.

It's interesting to become a Latino cultural ambassador when you're seven.

But Lin-Manuel had the opportunity to reconnect with his roots during the summers, when the Mirandas would return to Puerto Rico for a month. As big-city kids, Luz and Lin-Manuel enjoyed spending time exploring the island, discovering the unusual animals and plants of the Caribbean. Lin-Manuel was particularly fascinated by the morivoví plant, or touch-me-not, which curls its leaves when you touch them.

Later he would make his first movies in Puerto Rico, using a cheap video camera and staging battles between plastic soldiers in his grandparents' backyard.

A YOUNG SHOWMAN

Even when he was very young, Lin-Manuel was bursting with creative energy. His father recalls watching him singing in a choir, gesturing and acting out the song with such gusto that Luis knew then and there he'd be a star.

Another family story is that Lin-Manuel, in a piano recital at age seven, refused to stop playing because he so enjoyed the applause. He played every song he knew before finally allowing the next child to play.

Soon he was adding his own compositions to his recitals, along with funny explanations for his madcap ideas. For example, his first song—composed at age nine—was "Tarantella." It was, his own notes explain, "of Italian origin" and the corresponding "dance was believed to cure the poisonous bite of the tarantula spider." He wrote poems, too, with titles like "Gross Is Great!" and "Weird Stars." "Winter makes me feel like a green weirdo," goes one entire poem. In fourth grade, he wrote and recited a rap about "Jack and the Beanstalk."

Lin-Manuel also tried his hand at making movies. For a book report in grade school, he made a short movie about Jean Merrill's novel *The Pushcart War*, a futuristic fable set in New York City. The video included special effects, a score, and young Lin-Manuel playing several parts in costume. He also cast some of his family members in parts, showing an early talent for directing and producing.

His flair for the dramatic and his humor were also on display in his letters home from summer camp. "Dear Family, remember me?" he asked in one letter, and drew a picture of himself falling off a cabin roof to remind them. In other letters, he complained of scraped knees, malfunctioning electricity, and counselors who yelled too much. He missed his family and the big city he called home. Sometimes he wrote HELP or COME AND TAKE ME BACK TO NEW YORK in big letters at the bottom. One year, he faked an injury to go home early and had to stay in bed for a week to keep up the story. It was good practice for the future actor! It also worked: he was never sent to camp again.

Hi, Rember me? I'm the kid you ditched in the woods for a month! You know how we hardly ever go to mass? Well, I go every Sunday! Here's a picture to remind you of me:

⊰ A MOSTLY HAPPY CHILDHOOD ⊱

The Mirandas were a close and loving family, but a happy childhood isn't always an easy one. Lin-Manuel felt removed from the other children in the neighborhood because he didn't go to school there, and Hunter was challenging and put a lot of pressure on him. The students there called him Lin; he was always Lin-Manuel at home. It was like he was two different people.

Lin-Manuel had one of his worst experiences while he was in kindergarten: his mother had to tell him that a friend and classmate had drowned. Lin-Manuel was devastated. Most children don't have to think about death, or the shortness of life, but the incident opened young Lin-Manuel's eyes to mortality. He heard what he describes as "the ticking clock" whirring away the seconds of his life, a theme that appears in much of his creative work.

As a trained psychologist, his mother was able to help him work through his feelings about the loss of his friend. She told him that the difficult things he encountered in life would come in handy. If he was sad, he could remember later how it felt, and he could write about it or act it in a play.

Lin-Manuel took his mother's advice to heart
and invested his free time and energy in creating
things—poems, drawings, movies, and more. He soon
decided that his favorite medium was the stage,
especially after going to see his first Broadway play,
Les Misérables, at age seven.

BYE BYE BIRDIE, HELLO DREAMS

Every year, the Hunter College Elementary School's sixth-grade class put on a show for the rest of the school. Lin-Manuel had always wondered what show his class would do and whether he would have a part in it. When the big year came, the teachers decided to change the format of the show and instead do twenty-minute versions of six plays. Lin-Manuel landed the leading role in one: *Bye Bye Birdie*, the first rock-and-roll musical. He played Conrad Birdie, the central male character, who was based on Elvis Presley. Lin-Manuel spent hours practicing in front of the mirror, arching his eyebrows and curling his lip to look like the King of Rock and Roll.

Performing for everyone in the audience was the greatest moment of his life so far. *Why would anyone want to do anything else?* he thought. If he wasn't already convinced he had a life in theater, that event sealed his future.

CHAPTER 2

WAIT FOR IT

At the end of sixth grade, Lin-Manuel decided he wanted to be an actor. But in seventh grade, he started to feel shy about performing, and he stopped trying out for shows. Instead, he wrote poems in his notebooks and started writing his first play— a musical about an unchaperoned seventh-grade party called *Seven Minutes in Heaven*.

Around this time, he also began listening to hip-hop and rap music. Lin-Manuel listened to popular acts like the Beastie Boys, the Fat Boys, and the Notorious B.I.G. His school bus driver caught him up on older hip-hop, too, like the Sugarhill Gang and Boogie Down Productions.

Though Lin-Manuel enjoyed a variety of music genres, TV shows, movies, and musicals, he was aware that few people like himself and his parents ever played significant roles—Latino characters and artists were often portrayed as "bad guys." But Lin-Manuel found inspiration in the most famous Puerto Rican rapper at the time—Big Pun. He loved Big Pun's clever multisyllabic rhymes and wit. The rapper's name is itself a pun: it's short for "Big Punisher" but also refers to the wordplay in his lyrics. Lin-Manuel discovered new meanings every time he listened to Big Pun's songs.

In eighth grade, his class read the novel *The Chosen* by Chaim Potok. The book is about a Jewish boy coming of age and discovering a gift for analyzing sacred texts. Lin-Manuel was not Jewish, and not especially religious, but he connected with the main character's working-class New York life and restless mind. It became one of his favorite books. He decided that he would perform his class report on the book as a rap, even writing the parts for his group mates. His gift for crafting lyrics and performing caught the attention of the teacher, who then encouraged Lin-Manuel to share his talent with the rest of the school.

⋛ A TASTE FOR THE STAGE ⋛

Lin-Manuel joined the school's theater group, Brick Prison, which put on performances written and directed entirely by students. One musical skit Lin-Manuel wrote was about a preserved fetal pig coming back to life, inspired by biology classes where the students dissected pigs.

This could work as a play!

The following year, he began to audition for the bigger shows again. At first, he got small parts, including in the family drama *The Little Foxes* and the comedy *You Can't Take It with You*. But then he had the thrill of landing one of the major roles in *The Pirates of Penzance*. It was a big deal to Lin-Manuel because he beat out seniors for the part.

The Pirates of Penzance

Composer: Arthur Sullivan
Lyricist: W. S. Gilbert
Premiere: 1879

This opera tells the story of a young man who travels the world with a group of pirates. The best-known song is "I Am the Very Model of a Modern Major-General," which the comic characte Major-General Stanley uses to introduce himself It is a famous example of a "patter song," a comic song with rapidly spoken lines, often ful of tongue twisters and wordplay. Though patter is quite different musically from rap, the ener and wordplay are similar. Lin-Manuel riffs on the song "Modern Major-General" when George Washington introduces himself in *Hamilton*.

⋛ NO TIME FOR HANGING OUT ⋚

In classes, Lin-Manuel worked hard and got good grades, but his toughest subject was math, and he had to double down just to pass with a C. But one year in high school, he earned a trophy for improvement and relished it as much as any of the awards he's earned in show business since. It now sits on the shelf with his Tonys and Grammys.

The middle school and high school at Hunter were bigger and more diverse than the elementary school, so Lin-Manuel now had more friends. He was in a club for Latino students and in a group for Jewish students where he had the unusual title "secretary of not being Jewish." He joined the group because a lot of his friends were in it. Friends were as important to Lin-Manuel as music and family, and he loved collaborating in his creative work.

When he wasn't involved with live theater, he was making movies. His first listed film credit on the Internet Movie Database (IMDb) is as writer, director, producer, and costar of a horror movie called *Clayton's Friends*, made when he was sixteen years old. The plot follows a standard formula of teen horror flicks, with a group of friends disappearing one at a time.

Outside of school, too, Lin-Manuel was busy with many activities and his own creative endeavors, but he was also—along with his family—involved in the community. They volunteered their time at charities and other organizations. In election years, he and his father went from apartment building to apartment building to hand out pamphlets for candidates they thought would be best for the neighborhood. Sometimes it was boring, but both Luz and Lin-Manuel had learned from their parents that giving back to the community is important.

MEETING A FUTURE MENTOR

Perhaps the most important day in Lin-Manuel's high school life was when Stephen Sondheim spoke at Hunter College. Sondheim is thought by many to be the greatest Broadway composer and lyricist of the last fifty years. Like Lin-Manuel, Sondheim writes both the music and lyrics to his shows. His musicals, such as *Company* and *Sweeney Todd*, have been groundbreaking and challenging, and they often deal with dark subjects. One of the biggest shows of the 1980s, *Into the Woods*, even included some short raps, though it was far from a hip-hop score. But to Lin-Manuel, Sondheim's most important work was *West Side Story*.

West Side Story

Composer: Leonard Bernstein
Lyricist: Stephen Sondheim
Writer: Arthur Laurents
Premiere: 1957

Based on Shakespeare's *Romeo and Juliet*, the musical *West Side Story* is about the ill-fated love between two teenagers living in 1950s New York—a white boy named Tony and a Puerto Rican girl named Maria. They are kept apart by the rivalry between street gangs in their neighborhoods.

The show was a turning point in the history of musical theater because of its realistic themes, complex music, and high-energy dance scenes that mimicked street fights. The musical was made into a film in 1961; a new version is planned for 2020.

Lin-Manuel had been interested in *West Side Story* since he was in grade school, because it was the only famous musical to feature Puerto Rican characters. The first time he saw the movie version, he was struck that a musical could be about people like him and that anyone's story could matter.

By the time he was in high school, however, he had mixed feelings about the show. He still loved the music, of course, but it was discouraging that the only well-known play about Latino people portrayed them as gang members, reinforcing negative stereotypes. Worse was that in many productions the Puerto Rican characters were played by white actors. In the movie, white actors wore garish makeup to look Latino. Only one cast member—Rita Moreno—had Puerto Rican heritage.

Nevertheless, Lin-Manuel was thrilled to hear Sondheim speak and, later, to have the opportunity to direct *West Side Story* as a senior in high school. He would do it right, he decided. His father helped the actors master Puerto Rican accents, and Lin-Manuel brought authentic slang into the dialogue. He could not rewrite the play, but he could inject as much realism into the Puerto Rican characters as possible. He was too busy overseeing the production to play a part in the show himself.

⧿ TWO MUSICAL WORLDS ⧿

As a teenager, Lin-Manuel continued to be fascinated by both hip-hop music and Broadway musicals—two worlds that rarely overlapped.

One of the formative shows of his lifetime came out when he was fourteen: *Rent*, by Jonathan Larson. It would become one of his favorite shows, and Larson one of his biggest influences.

IMPORTANT INFLUENCES

<u>Rent</u>

Composer: Jonathan Larson
Lyricist: Jonathan Larson
Writer: Jonathan Larson
Premiere: 1996

Rent is an imaginative reinvention of Puccini's opera *La Bohème* with a rock soundtrack. The pl shows interconnected stories of young, poor artists living and working in New York City at the peak of the AIDS epidemic. Perhaps the mos important musical of the 1990s, *Rent* won sever awards, ran for twelve years on Broadway, and toured the country. It was also adapted into film with much of the original cast.

Rent included the song "Today 4 U," with rap lines woven into the lyrics. Although it still wasn't the kind of hip-hop musical Lin-Manuel would write, it was proof that such a mix could be successful. And just as musicals occasionally worked in a little rap, rap music sometimes worked in samples of show tunes. One of the biggest hits of the 1990s was Jay-Z's "Hard Knock Life (Ghetto Anthem)," which sampled a bright musical refrain from *Annie* and blended it seamlessly with Jay-Z's masterful wordplay. These examples of the melding of hip-hop and show tunes helped Lin-Manuel see how the two forms could work together. After all, both genres were about telling stories through music.

Another of Lin-Manuel's favorite musicians, though a less obvious influence, was comedian Alfred "Weird Al" Yankovic, whose best-known songs are parodies of pop hits. Weird Al used the same wit and ingenious rhymes Lin-Manuel admired in musicals and hip-hop.

Lin-Manuel's interests in rap music, show tunes, and musical parodies might seem incompatible, but his interests had a common thread: the well-crafted line. He valued good lyrics and appreciated that they could take shape in many different genres of music. For him, there was no inconsistency at all. Pop, hip-hop, and show tunes were the soundtrack of his life.

CHAPTER 3

HISTORY IS HAPPENING IN MANHATTAN

After graduating from high school in 1998, Lin-Manuel was accepted at Wesleyan University, a prestigious college in Middletown, Connecticut, about a two-hour drive from Manhattan. It was close enough for him to go back to New York when he was homesick.

As at Hunter, Lin-Manuel was a hard worker and a good student. He originally wanted to major in film and theater but quickly abandoned film to focus completely on stage productions. He loved the "instant gratification" of planning and performing in a show on a tight schedule, and the thrill of hearing the audience's applause when all the hard work paid off. The theater department also financed student shows, whereas student filmmakers had to come up with their own money to make their films.

The theater major required a wide range of coursework on the history of theater, reading and analyzing a variety of plays, and behind-the-scenes work. The program also required a "capstone" work in the final year—usually writing and staging a play.

In his freshman year, Lin-Manuel starred in *Jesus Christ Superstar*, but his desire to write his own plays and music was growing. For one thing, few plays had roles meant for people of color, like him. For another, he wanted to write music that felt more contemporary and relevant. He also knew he would have to stage an original play to complete the program, and was consumed with what that play would be.

I want to write and star in my own play.

⋛ BACK IN "THE HEIGHTS" ⋛

About the time Lin-Manuel started college, his father
helped set up a newspaper, the *Manhattan Times*,
that covered upper Manhattan, including Inwood and
Washington Heights. The newspaper ran articles on
local issues in both English and Spanish. During the
summer, Lin-Manuel returned home and worked for
the paper.

The job brought him into Washington Heights, the
heart of the Latino community in New York City.
Throughout school, Lin-Manuel had been removed
from his own community of Latino people, but now
he was in the thick of it, talking to people as he
researched stories. He wrote columns about the
neighborhood and penned restaurant reviews. Many
of the people he met were from the Spanish-speaking
islands of the Caribbean: Puerto Rico, Cuba, and the
Dominican Republic, but there were also Orthodox
Jewish people, African Americans, and other groups.
Lin-Manuel heard all sorts of music blasting from
radios and boom boxes. He began to envision a musical
set in the neighborhood, with the same mixture of
voices and musical styles.

The Sounds of Washington Heights

In addition to rap and pop, Lin-Manuel heard:

▶ Klezmer: Jewish folk music from Europe

▶ Soul: African American pop music derived from blues and gospel

▶ Salsa: a blend of pop with traditional Latin and Caribbean musical styles

▶ Merengue: the traditional music of the Dominican Republic

▶ Reggaeton: a mix of modern rap music with traditional Caribbean and Latin styles

⋚ THE BEGINNINGS OF A SHOW ⋚

In Lin-Manuel's second year at college, he transferred to a dormitory with other Latino students at Wesleyan, nicknamed La Casa—Spanish for "the home." This experience, along with his summer job, gave him ideas for the new musical forming in his mind that incorporated the sounds and stories of Latin culture at its core. It wouldn't be a show about Latino people in gangs, but one about the people he knew and loved.

He finished a first draft of *In the Heights* in three weeks and convinced a student theater group, Second Stage, to perform it. It was a one-act play and was less than an hour long, with fewer and less developed characters than the full-blown musical it would become years later. Lin-Manuel describes that first draft as a simple love story.

⸗ THE DAY THE WORLD CHANGED ⸗

Shortly after his senior year started, Lin-Manuel had a Tuesday morning with no classes. He stopped in a record store to buy the newest album by Bob Dylan, which had come out that day. He noticed that the store clerk looked strange, and so Lin-Manuel asked him what was wrong. The clerk told him devastating news: two airplanes had crashed into the twin towers of the World Trade Center. The buildings were in lower Manhattan, about twelve miles south of Lin-Manuel's home. He couldn't process the news.

He hurried back to La Casa and tried to call home, but the lines were jammed and he couldn't get through. He turned on the TV and saw both towers smoking, then falling. Afternoon classes were canceled.

As the morning wore on, his housemates gathered to watch the news. One had a brother who worked at the World Trade Center, but he'd called in sick that day. Sadly, another friend's father died in the attack. The entire nation was affected, but for the people of New York City, it was a personal tragedy—everyone had a friend, a neighbor, or a relative who worked in or near the buildings. It would be many anxious hours, or even days, of waiting to learn who had been spared by chance, who had fled in the nick of time, and who was gone.

Lin-Manuel had been busy with his own studies and creative projects, trying to finish college, but now saw himself in the bigger picture of history. He heard the "ticking clock" he'd heard since kindergarten. He knew that whatever plans he made, his life—or the world— could change in a heartbeat.

"'I imagine death so much it feels more like a memory.' . . . It's what I feel I have most in common with Hamilton: the ticking clock of mortality is loud in both our ears, and it sets us to work."

YOUNG, SCRAPPY, AND HUNGRY

After he graduated in 2002, Lin-Manuel wasn't sure what to do with himself. He wanted to write and star in musicals, but he also had to make a living, and he knew that a career in show business would be both a long struggle and a long shot. An old saying is "There's a broken heart for every light on Broadway."

He returned home to Inwood and worked various temporary and part-time jobs to make ends meet. He became a substitute English teacher at his old school, Hunter College High School, and continued working for his father's newspaper. He tried out for voice work in radio commercials but was usually only asked to read for commercials for tacos or other Latin products. Even surrendering to stereotypes, he didn't get any of the jobs.

Lin-Manuel was struck by the changes to the Washington Heights neighborhood since he'd first started working for the *Manhattan Times* a few years before. The entire city was still recovering from the attacks in September 2001. But New York City was also undergoing another transition. For decades, white people had been moving out of the city and into the suburbs, leaving behind racially diverse but often poor neighborhoods. Now younger, wealthier people were moving back in. Upscale businesses and more expensive housing were cropping up. Rent prices started to skyrocket, driving long-time residents out.

This change inspired Lin-Manuel to write about Washington Heights as more than a setting. He wanted to celebrate it as a unique community that was disappearing, and to highlight this threat. His original version of *In the Heights* had been a simple love story, told in one act. He now decided to bring in more characters and story lines to show a wider range of people and experiences.

⹂ HIS FATHER'S BLESSING ⹂

After a year of substitute teaching at Hunter, Lin-Manuel was offered a permanent position there. He was torn between having the security of a regular job and having the time to pursue his creative ambitions. To help him decide, his father wrote him a letter encouraging him to follow his dreams—even if it meant saying no to a full-time job. Luis admitted it wasn't typical parental advice, but he himself had left a good job in Puerto Rico to risk moving to New York City. He had taken a big chance and had no regrets.

So Lin-Manuel declined the full-time job at Hunter, though he continued to teach as a substitute part-time and took other temp jobs while revising and developing *In the Heights*.

⋛ FREESTYLE LOVE SUPREME ⋛

Lin-Manuel also founded an improv group called
Freestyle Love Supreme with two fellow Wesleyan
alumni: Thomas "Tommy" Kail and Anthony Veneziale.
They had seen the one-act version of *In the Heights*
at Wesleyan in 2000 and wanted Lin-Manuel to join
them. Freestyle Love Supreme performed in a variety
of clubs and small theaters in the city. They made
up on-the-spot raps based on suggestions from the
audience. At first, Lin-Manuel was terrified.

You learn to just trust
your gut, and you jump
out of the plane, and you
build the parachute on
the way down.

But over time, he gained confidence and enjoyed
the connections and energy among the performers.
He especially had creative chemistry with Tommy.

Tommy was good at piecing things together, and he showed Lin-Manuel how various parts of *In the Heights* could be better woven together to improve the show. Tommy would eventually be the director of both *In the Heights* and *Hamilton*.

Tommy Kail

Thomas "Tommy" Kail was born on January 20, 1977, in Alexandria, Virginia. Like Lin-Manuel, he attended Wesleyan University, but they didn't know each other at the time. He received Tony nominations for his work on *In the Heights* and *Hamilton*, and won for the latter. His other plays include *Broke-ology*, *Lombardi*, and a reprise of *The Wiz*. In 2019, he and playwright Steven Levenson cocreated *Fosse/Verdon*, a TV series about legendary choreographer Bob Fosse and his creative and romantic partner, Gwen Verdon.

⤜ SOUL MATES ⤛

By 2005, social networking sites were starting to
take off, and Lin-Manuel signed up for Facebook.
He reached out to people from college and Hunter
in an effort to reconnect with old friends. During this
time, he came across the profile of Vanessa Nadal,
a girl he'd gone to high school with and had a crush
on but didn't know that well. He saw that after high
school she had gone to the Massachusetts Institute of
Technology and majored in chemical engineering, and
she was now working in research and development for a
pharmaceutical company. Her page listed that she liked
salsa and hip-hop, so Lin-Manuel sent her a message
and told her about Freestyle Love Supreme. He wasn't
sure if she would show up, but a few nights later, he saw
her in the audience. They talked after the show and
hit it off, especially when he found out she also liked
musicals.

For his second date with Vanessa, Lin-Manuel
wanted to impress her, so he asked Alex Lacamoire—
a new friend and musician he'd been introduced to
by his Freestyle Love Supreme castmates—to get
him tickets to the hottest show in town. The play was

Wicked, a retelling of *The Wizard of Oz* from the witch's point of view. Alex was an associate conductor of the musical. Vanessa was impressed. The two kept dating and fell in love.

⇒ NO OVERNIGHT SUCCESS STORY ⇒

For the next few years, Lin-Manuel supported himself with substitute teaching and occasional songwriting gigs, including music for local commercials. Many were political ads that came through his father's connections. Lin-Manuel would compose "mood music"—dark and foreboding, as the ad discussed the candidate's opponent, changing to sunny and bright when the ad turned to the candidate.

He performed with Freestyle Love Supreme often and continued rewriting and revising *In the Heights* with Tommy. He wrote five drafts, fleshing out the characters and story. With each draft, he and the group of actors would read through the script at a small theater owned by a fellow Wesleyan alumni. In college, Lin-Manuel had chosen live theater over film because he wanted "instant gratification," but now he was learning it wasn't quite that straightforward. It might only take a few months to stage a musical in high school or college, but if you wanted to get to Broadway, the process was much longer.

Sometimes a star like Lin-Manuel is called an "overnight success," but the truth is that "overnight successes" are usually several years in the making. These are the years that Lin-Manuel truly became a professional, polishing both his writing and performance skills. He worked other odd jobs when he needed to, but enjoyed the gift of his father's blessing: he put his creative work first.

CHAPTER 4

EVERYBODY'S GOT A DREAM

As Lin-Manuel and Tommy continued to work on
In the Heights, they knew they needed somebody to
help orchestrate and arrange the music. They turned to
Alex Lacamoire, who shared their enthusiasm for *In the
Heights*. As a Cuban American, he had an immediate
connection with Lin-Manuel on the story and music.
Because Alex was so busy with *Wicked*, much of the
music for *In the Heights* was done backstage at the
Gershwin Theatre, where *Wicked* was showing. It was
the only way for Lin-Manuel and Alex to meet and
work together.

KEY COLLABORATOR

Alex Lacamoire

Alex Lacamoire was born
in Los Angeles on May 24,
1975. As a child, he was
diagnosed with partial
hearing loss. His family
moved to Miami when he
was young, where he began

playing piano at age four. Despite his hearing problem, he was considered a piano prodigy. He decided he wanted to make a living in music. He went to the prestigious Berklee College of Music in Boston, Massachusetts, and after graduation helped arrange, conduct, and perform music for hit Broadway shows like *Legally Blonde* and *Wicked*, as well as the off-Broadway *Bat Boy*. He has received Tony Awards for his work on *In the Heights* and *Hamilton*.

Now that Tommy and Alex were partners, the key pieces were almost in place for Lin-Manuel to make *In the Heights* become a reality. Another big break was finding producers—financial backers—for the show. The producers for *In the Heights* included Jeffrey Seller and Kevin McCollum, who had backed other experimental theater productions including *Rent* and the surprise hit *Avenue Q*, a musical puppet show. Now they were willing to take a chance on *In the Heights*.

However, Jeffrey and Kevin thought *In the Heights* needed an experienced playwright, so they advised hiring Quiara Alegría Hudes to write the nonmusical parts of the script, called "the book" in theater terminology.

Quiara Alegría Hudes

Born in 1977, Quiara Alegría Hudes was raised in Philadelphia by Puerto Rican parents. She studied music at Yale University in New Haven, Connecticut, then got a master of fine arts in playwriting from Brown University in Providence, Rhode Island. *In the Heights* was her breakout work. She has since won a Pulitzer Prize for the play *Water by the Spoonful*. Her most recent work is a collaboration with Lin-Manuel Miranda on the movie *Vivo*.

At last, after years of redrafting, the full version of the new *In the Heights* had its first run at the Eugene O'Neill Theater Center in Waterford, Connecticut, from July 23 through July 31, 2005. Many shows are "tested" in theaters outside New York City as the developers work out the kinks. Although Lin-Manuel would later star in the show, he did not perform in this production. He wanted to focus on perfecting the music. Usnavi, the main character, was played by Javier Muñoz.

WHAT'S THE STORY?

In the Heights

Composers: Lin-Manuel Miranda and Alex Lacamoire

Lyricist: Lin-Manuel Miranda

Writer: Quiara Alegría Hudes

Premiere: 2005

Usnavi is a young store owner living in Washington Heights. He dreams of moving back to the Dominican Republic, where his family is from, but doesn't have the money to do so. He and his friends in the community are all struggling with the rising price of rent and the threat of local businesses closing. When Usnavi realizes he's sold a winning lottery ticket, he knows somebody's dreams are about to come true—but whose?

Audiences enjoyed the musical, but it only ran for two weekends. Afterward, Lin-Manuel and his collaborators continued to polish the show before it opened at the 37 Arts Theatre in New York—off-Broadway—in early 2007. It was exhausting work, and sometimes Lin-Manuel would sleep for a few hours at the rehearsal space instead of going home.

In the off-Broadway production, Lin-Manuel took on the starring role of Usnavi. The show got rave reviews, and at the end of the five-month run, the producers felt it was finally ready for Broadway. His dream was slowly coming true, but Lin-Manuel was too busy to relish it. He turned his attention again to the music, continuing to work on the lyrics and improve the melodies.

In the Heights debuted on Broadway in February 2008 at the Richard Rodgers Theatre. While critics lauded the music and performances, they saved their highest praise for Lin-Manuel himself, whose charm and enthusiasm carried the show. It was extraordinary for one person to write the music and lyrics *and* star in the show, and most critics saw a special quality in Lin-Manuel.

"If you stroll down to the Richard Rodgers Theatre, where the spirited musical *In the Heights* opened on Sunday night, you'll discover a singular new sensation, Lin-Manuel Miranda, commanding the spotlight as if he were born in the wings."
—*The New York Times*

IN THE HEIGHTS IN THE HEIGHTS

Even better than the good reviews was the impact
of the musical on the neighborhood where it's
set—Washington Heights. Although some critics
complained that the musical glossed over realities of
the neighborhood, for people in the community that
wasn't the point. It was a chance to see themselves
represented, and as more than the knife-fighting
hoodlums in *West Side Story*.

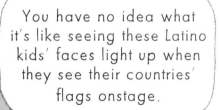

You have no idea what
it's like seeing these Latino
kids' faces light up when
they see their countries'
flags onstage.

⟩ LIFE AFTER STARDOM ⟨

After the first year, Lin-Manuel left the part of Usnavi to Javier Muñoz and started to pursue other work while *In the Heights* continued to thrive. It was the biggest turning point in his career so far. Although he wasn't the international celebrity he would become with *Hamilton*, he began to get regular work in entertainment.

Perhaps the most exciting opportunity was an invitation to write Spanish-language lyrics for a Broadway revival of *West Side Story*. Arthur Laurents, one of the original creators of the play in 1959, was directing the revival and wanted to have the Puerto Rican characters speaking Spanish among themselves. One of the producers recommended that Lin-Manuel write the new dialogue and music, an obvious choice given the success of *In the Heights*.

Lin-Manuel's admiration for *West Side Story* had deepened since he directed the performance in high school. He particularly appreciated Leonard Bernstein's ability to weave different voices and styles into a rich and coherent whole. Lin-Manuel and Alex had drawn inspiration from it while developing the music for *In the Heights*. So of course he was thrilled by the opportunity to help with a reprise, one that involved two of the original creators, and that would give him a chance to show a more realistic, firsthand depiction of Puerto Rican people.

But it was a new challenge for Lin-Manuel, who had never written entirely in Spanish, even though he had grown up bilingual and woven Spanish lyrics into many of the songs for *In the Heights*.

It was the hardest bilingual crossword puzzle I've ever done.

He wrote original lyrics with his own imagery rather than an exact translation of the original words, but Stephen Sondheim did require that he keep the rhythm and rhymes of the original to fit the music. Though famous for being highly demanding, Sondheim was impressed by Lin-Manuel's translations.

Where Maria originally sings that she feels "pretty and bright" in "I Feel Pretty," one of the best-known songs in the original, in Lin-Manuel's Spanish version, "Siento Hermosa," she sings that she feels so pretty she can fly and will outshine the stars. Lin-Manuel's lyrics were considered a high point of the production, more creative than a word-for-word translation would be.

The revival ran for two years and led to a lot of shared admiration between Lin-Manuel and Stephen Sondheim. While Sondheim recognized Lin-Manuel as an innovator, one who would be a serious game changer on Broadway, what really impressed him was the younger man's deep knowledge and respect for the past.

"Lin knows where musical theater comes from, and he cares about where it comes from."
—Stephen Sondheim

The legendary composer would be an early champion of *Hamilton*, and now reviews and gives feedback on Lin-Manuel's new work. In turn, Lin-Manuel would star in a two-week reprise of Sondheim's *Merrily We Roll Along* in February 2012 as a favor to his mentor. Sondheim hoped Lin-Manuel's star power would help the revival of a musical that had been one of Sondheim's rare flops. Indeed, Lin-Manuel brought "original verve and credibility" to the show, a *New York Times* reviewer wrote.

A BUSY MAN ON A BREAK

During this time, Lin-Manuel also started doing more acting work. His first official credit was for a single scene in the HBO series *The Sopranos* in 2007, in which he plays a bellman. Lin-Manuel admits that he makes a minor flub in the scene, glancing down for the mark on the floor to make sure he's in the right place.

In 2008, he performed a song from *In the Heights* on the Tony Awards show, and later he picked up the award for Best Score—it was his first Tony Award, but not his last. Lin-Manuel freestyle-rapped his acceptance speech, rattling off rhymes to thank everyone involved in the show, as well as Vanessa, his parents, and his *abuela,* who inspired one of the characters.

He ended the speech by acknowledging his fellow Latinos, waving a Puerto Rican flag—imitating a scene in the play—as the audience applauded. Later, *In the Heights* won Best Musical, the most anticipated award of the night. After the producers gave a quick speech, the cast hoisted Lin-Manuel onto their shoulders. Lin-Manuel was now officially a big name on Broadway.

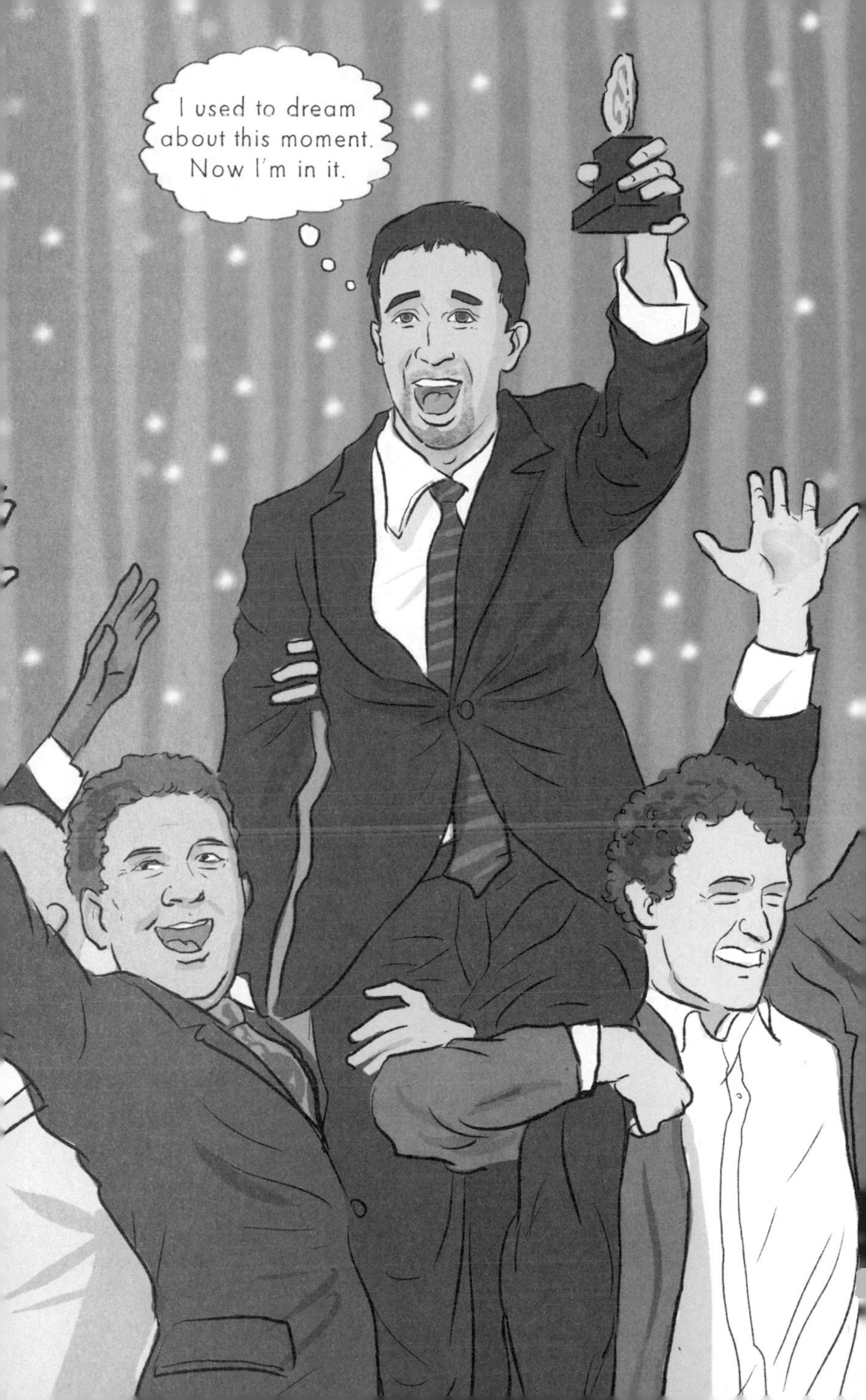
I used to dream about this moment. Now I'm in it.

A bigger TV role came up the following year. One of the executive producers of the hit TV show *House, M.D.* had seen *In the Heights* and wanted to write a part for Lin-Manuel. As a fan of the show, Lin-Manuel quickly accepted and cleared his calendar to go to Los Angeles and shoot his scenes. He played the offbeat, manic hospital roommate of the star of the show, Hugh Laurie, who was the most watched and highest-paid actor in television at the time. Because the part was written especially for Lin-Manuel, it even included some freestyle rapping.

Lin-Manuel continued to play several minor parts over the next year, including on *Sesame Street*, where he performed the theme song for a segment called "Murray Has a Little Lamb." In another skit, he plays a real estate agent who only sells homes to birds and tries to convince Big Bird to migrate south for the winter. He also had parts on *The Electric Company* and *Do No Harm*.

In November 2010, he resumed the role of Usnavi for a week in Puerto Rico. Lin-Manuel was thrilled to perform in his parents' homeland. He was received there as a hero. At the end of each performance, audience members would wave small Puerto Rican flags in celebration of the musical.

⧘ TO THE GROOM! TO THE BRIDE! ⧗

On September 5, 2010, Lin-Manuel and Vanessa were married. In the lead-up to the big day, Lin-Manuel practiced a song in secret with their family and friends to surprise Vanessa at the reception. It started as a simple wedding speech but quickly turned into a fully choreographed musical number from *Fiddler on the Roof*. The video became a viral sensation with millions of views and thousands of comments.

WRITING LIKE HE'S RUNNING OUT OF TIME

Though he was busy acting, Lin-Manuel was always writing, too. His next two projects were unique challenges.

The first was a stage adaptation of *Bring It On*, a movie about competitive cheerleading. Lin-Manuel helped compose the music and lyrics, since the writers of the show wanted a contemporary soundtrack with hip-hop and rock elements. Unlike Lin-Manuel's other work, the show is as much about dancing as it is music, incorporating impressive cheerleading stunts into the dance sequences. They were choreographed by Andy Blankenbuehler, who had worked on *In the Heights* and would later work on *Hamilton*.

KEY COLLABORATOR

Andy Blankenbuehler

Andy Blankenbuehler was born on March 7, 1970, in Cincinnati, Ohio. He was a dancer on Broadway throughout the 1990s, appearing in hit shows like *Guys and Dolls* and *Fosse*. *In the Heights* was his first job as choreographer, the person who composes the dance sequences for a show. Besides his collaborations with Lin-Manuel Miranda (*In the Heights*, *Bring It On*, and *Hamilton*), he has choreographed *9 to 5*, *Waiting for the Moon*, and many other shows, as well as the movie version of *Cats*. He has been nominated for the Tony Award for Best Choreography five times.

Bring It On was unusual because it was first performed in Atlanta, Georgia, and played in several other cities before making its Broadway debut in 2012. It got good reviews, particularly for Lin-Manuel Miranda's libretto (lyrics). The producers' decision to include hip-hop in the show was proof of the immediate impact Lin-Manuel's new style was already having on Broadway. The show, with its mix of rap-battle-style lyrics and choreography inspired by cheering routines, was described as "dazzling" in the *New York Times* review. The show was nominated for Tony Awards for Best Musical and Best Choreography, among others, but lost both to Cyndi Lauper's *Kinky Boots*.

Bring It On

Composers: Lin-Manuel Miranda and Tom Kitt

Lyricists: Amanda Green and Lin-Manuel Miranda

Writer: Jeff Whitty

Premiere: 2012

Campbell Davis is the cheer captain at a rich high school. She has the perfect life, the perfect boyfriend, and a prize-winning cheer team. Suddenly, though, Campbell is transferred to a school in a tougher neighborhood that doesn't even have a cheer team. She forms and trains a new squad to take on her old team in city competitions.

Alongside his other work, Lin-Manuel also wrote a theme song, "Bigger!," for the 2013 Tonys, which was performed by the host, Neil Patrick Harris. The lyrics are filled with joking references to the popular shows of the year—including *Bring It On*, with the cheerleader-dancers onstage. The song later won an Emmy Award for Outstanding Original Music and Lyrics in a TV program. So even though Lin-Manuel didn't win any Tonys that night, he still came out a winner.

Later that year, Lin-Manuel made a guest appearance on the TV show *How I Met Your Mother*, which also starred Neil Patrick Harris. Like Lin-Manuel's role on *House*, the character was written with him in mind. He plays a young man on a train who speaks entirely in freestyle rap.

Lin-Manuel also wrote a one-act musical called *21 Chump Street*. It was part of a stage show based on the nonfiction radio program *This American Life*. The show mixed journalism with musical theater, telling true stories through song. As the lyricist, Lin-Manuel worked as much as possible with quotes from the original radio story, figuring out how to make the words melodic and find the rhymes. After it premiered on June 7, 2014, at the Brooklyn Academy of Music, reviewers said that his was the best section in the *This American Life* stage show and that Lin-Manuel's skill at weaving real dialogue into lyrics was impressive and witty.

Yet another project Lin-Manuel worked on was a brief reprise of the play *Tick, Tick . . . BOOM!* in 2014. Originally a one-act, one-man show written by and starring Jonathan Larson, the creator of *Rent*, it was revised as a three-act play with three characters.

The show is very personal, exploring Larson's ambitions and anxiety, and Lin-Manuel has said it has been a big influence on his own creative process. Leslie Odom Jr. also starred in the show, beginning the creative partnership he and Lin-Manuel would bring to *Hamilton*, when Leslie took on the role of Aaron Burr, Hamilton's rival.

Lin-Manuel then made his first leap into a major motion picture by writing two songs for *Star Wars: The Force Awakens*, "Dobra Doompa" and "Jabba Flow." Both were inspired by the cantina song in the original *Star Wars* movie. The vocals were by Lin-Manuel himself and the director J. J. Abrams, though synthesized to sound more alien and barely recognizable.

⋛ HAVING A BLAST ⋛

With his name on three successful musicals and regular appearances on television and Broadway, Lin-Manuel had fully proven himself as a multitalented entertainer, one who could write, direct, sing, and act. He was also clearly having fun. From Sondheim to *Star Wars*, he was working with his heroes and getting his name in the credits of his favorite movie franchises and TV shows. He was having a blast!

But perhaps the biggest career-changing moment came in the midst of all these projects, when Lin-Manuel was neither onstage nor on camera. In 2008, he and Vanessa were taking a well-earned vacation to a resort in Mexico. He wanted a book to read and decided on Ron Chernow's biography of Alexander Hamilton. It was an unplanned choice, and he surely didn't know the book would change his life, let alone American theater. He didn't know anything about Hamilton at the time except that he was on the ten-dollar bill.

Surprisingly, Lin-Manuel was immediately pulled into Hamilton's rags-to-riches story. As part of a revolutionary circle in New York City, with intense energy and a way with words, the character struck a deep chord within him. By the time he was on chapter two, he was already imagining the founding fathers as hip-hop characters.

CHAPTER 5

SOMETHING TO PROVE

Lin-Manuel was nervous the day Ron Chernow showed up for a matinee performance of *In the Heights*. It was the middle of 2008, near the end of the first year of *In the Heights* on Broadway. After finishing the biography of Alexander Hamilton, Lin-Manuel had invited the author to a show and asked him to meet afterward. Chernow was curious but not as shocked as he might have been. Indeed, he'd heard rumors that the rising Broadway star had been seen reading his book and that it had dog-eared corners and scribbles on the pages.

Lin-Manuel performed the show as always but felt butterflies. Other cast members must have been confused. Why would Lin-Manuel be nervous that a historian was in the audience?

I hope Ron enjoys the show. . . .

While Alexander Hamilton's story is history and belongs to everyone, Lin-Manuel had drawn his inspiration from Ron's book, and he wanted the biographer's permission to adapt the book into a musical, and his help getting the details right. Of course, Lin-Manuel would need to change a few things to fit an eight-hundred-page book into a two-and-a-half-hour musical, but he wanted to be true to the larger-than-life characters.

IMPORTANT INFLUENCES

Alexander Hamilton

Alexander Hamilton was born on January 11, 1755, in Charlestown on the island of Nevis, in the Caribbean. He became an orphan at a young age but was taken in by a merchant and later sent to New York for his education after villagers recognized his intelligence and potential and raised the funds for him.

America was a group of colonies of Great Britain at the time, but there was revolution in the air—many Americans wanted independence. In New York, Hamilton met several important people key to the revolution, including Aaron Burr.

Like Hamilton, Burr was an orphan. But instead of hitting it off, the two men rubbed each other the wrong way and became political rivals. Hamilton soon became the right-hand man to General George Washington, commander-in-chief of the Continental army. Burr was bitterly jealous.

In the city, Hamilton also met the wealthy and powerful Schuyler family and got engaged to Elizabeth "Eliza" Schuyler.

After the US won its independence at the end of the war in 1783, Hamilton continued to thrive in politics. He helped write the US Constitution, which established the new US government and laws, and later the Federalist Papers, a series of documents outlining a vision for the new American republic. As the first secretary of the treasury, his theories shaped the American economy we know today.

However, Hamilton then became involved in a scandal that stained his reputation and marriage. This was followed by the tragic death of his son in a duel at age 19—one he entered to defend his father against a verbal attack.

Meanwhile, Burr decided to run for president against Thomas Jefferson in the election of 1800. Hamilton publicly supported Jefferson, who ended up winning. This made the relationship between Hamilton and Burr even worse. In 1804, Burr ran for governor of New York. He suffered a humiliating defeat. Burr blamed his loss on Hamilton's public criticisms of him and demanded a duel. On July 11, 1804, Burr and Hamilton met in Weehawken, New Jersey, for a duel. Burr shot and killed Hamilton.

One of Hamilton's greatest legacies is the Doctrine of Implied Powers, the argument that the federal government could use powers not specifically granted in the Constitution for the "general welfare" of the people, such as passing civil rights laws.

If Ron Chernow hadn't liked *In the Heights* and hadn't thought a musical adaptation made any sense, the new show bubbling in Lin-Manuel's brain might never have happened.

Fortunately, Ron *did* like *In the Heights*, though he wasn't usually a fan of musicals. He was skeptical when Lin-Manuel told him that he wanted to use hip-hop lyrics in an adaptation of his biography of Alexander Hamilton. Still, he was intrigued. While he had never imagined his work as a musical, it was an opportunity to bring Hamilton's story to a wider audience. If nothing else, Chernow was won over by the young man's earnestness. He also saw that Lin-Manuel would be a perfect fit to play Hamilton—his slight build and boyish enthusiasm, and the way he spoke in inspired bursts, were exactly how he imagined the American founding father. While the musical wouldn't necessarily be a faithful recounting of events, maybe it would lead people to take more interest in history. Ron agreed to come on board as a historical consultant. Lin-Manuel was emboldened and encouraged by Ron's tentative approval and continued to work on the project, spending several months on the first song, "Alexander Hamilton."

A "MUSICAL ALBUM"

The next test for the material came at the White House in May 2009. Until that point, Lin-Manuel had shared the song only with Vanessa and Alex, who played the piano at the performance.

Though Lin-Manuel now says he might have scrapped the entire project if the song had gone over poorly at the showcase, we'll never know if he could have let it go. But seeing the president and First Lady jump to their feet that night and hearing the applause from the whole room gave him a jolt of confidence.

It would take years to turn that one song into a complete musical. He spent an entire year on the song "My Shot." He once posted on Twitter that he'd spent a whole day on one rhyme!

Even then, though, Lin-Manuel still wasn't sure it would ever be a *show*. He had completed and recorded a collection of songs, but he knew all too well that a Broadway show needed financial backing, a cast, and collaborators. It was possible that nobody would take a chance on such a strange idea.

He frequently thought of Andrew Lloyd Webber and Tim Rice, who released some of their early musicals as record albums to help find the interest and financial backing for a full show. *Jesus Christ Superstar* and *Evita* were two "musical albums" that went on to be very successful shows. Knowing that he and Alex could at least do that much, Lin-Manuel kept writing. He kicked things into higher gear after Tommy Kail pointed out that if he only wrote two songs in two years, they would be old men before he was done!

While he was making guest appearances on TV shows, composing songs for *Bring It On* and Spanish lyrics for *West Side Story*, even while he was on his honeymoon, Lin-Manuel was writing lyrics into notebooks, discussing the music with Alex and the story with Ron, trying to fit all the characters, events, and inspired wordplay together like a puzzle.

⋛ THE HAMILTON MIXTAPE ⋛

On January 11, 2012, the 255th birthday of Alexander
Hamilton, Lin-Manuel performed a handful of songs
at Lincoln Center in Manhattan, for the American
Songbook series. He was aided by Alex and Tommy
and a handful of actors from *In the Heights*. The
concept was called *The Hamilton Mixtape*. Though not
many of these singers would star in the final version
of *Hamilton*, they were all black and Latino singers.
Having people of color in the key roles had always
been a central part of Lin-Manuel's vision. There were
many reasons for the choice, the main ones being that
Lin-Manuel wanted to create opportunities for actors
of color, and he felt that black and Latino performers
could sing the hip-hop lyrics more authentically.

The cast and creators were stunned to find a packed
house and a lot of reporters. The performance itself
was electric.

"I saw the audience just quivering. You
could feel the hairs on the backs of
everyone's necks were standing up."
—Tommy Kail

The interest in the new musical was picking up momentum. The reviews of the performance helped the surge of interest.

"Is [it] a future Broadway musical? A concept album? A multimedia extravaganza in search of a platform? Does it even matter? What it is, is hot."
—The New York Times

On July 27, 2013, the same group who'd appeared at Lincoln Center presented the entire first act of the show—still called The Hamilton Mixtape— at Vassar College's Powerhouse Theater in Poughkeepsie, New York. The theater runs special "readings," where audiences can see plays in progress, and performers can test their material. There were no costumes or staging at this point, just Alex on the piano and a small group of performers singing and rapping.

By a stroke of luck, there was a special festival in town honoring Alexander Hamilton that weekend. Needless to say, Hamilton scholars—including Ron Chernow—packed the theater to hear the new songs.

The performance generated lots of excitement, and it became clear that *Hamilton* could not only be a musical, it could be a big hit. In light of this, the producers who financed *In the Heights* decided to take a chance on *Hamilton*, too, and Jeffrey Seller convinced Lin-Manuel that it was time to start preparing for an off-Broadway premiere. They found an eager partner in the Public Theater, which had hosted the off-Broadway previews of *In the Heights* and had been hoping to get Lin-Manuel's next show ever since. The artistic director there, Oskar Eustis, was particularly keen to be involved after seeing the Lincoln Center and Vassar College performances. Jeffrey knew people would associate the Public and Oskar with experimental and up-and-coming theater and thought this was the best way to brand the show.

"[The Public is] the quintessential New York downtown theater laboratory." —Jeffrey Seller

⋛ PREPARING FOR PREMIERE ⋚

After the decision to go off-Broadway, Lin-Manuel quickly realized he needed to get on with writing the rest of the show—the whole of the second act! Jeffrey offered his home in the Hamptons as a place for Lin-Manuel to go and work without any distractions. Vanessa, too, encouraged Lin-Manuel in his writing. From the moment he'd looked up from Chernow's biography and said, "I think I can make this a hip-hop musical," and she responded, "That sounds cool," Vanessa had aided his creative vision. She would often book trips abroad—to Spain, Puerto Rico, the Dominican Republic, and other places—to get him away from everyday life so he could focus on his work.

By 2014, the first full draft of the musical was complete. A short run of performances was scheduled at the 52nd Street Project in New York to gauge audience reaction before the off-Broadway premiere. This would be the first time performing both acts in front of an audience—and in costume. Paul Tazewell, the costume designer, had decided to use period dress from the neck down, reflecting the historical aspects of the play, and modern styling from the neck up, to complement the contemporary elements. The first of the four performances, which all seated only 150 people, was on Friday, May 9. By Monday morning, *Hamilton* was all anyone in New York was talking about.

The main thing audiences took away from the performances was the effect of seeing actors of color portraying the founding fathers and winning American independence. As the creators have often summarized:

"This is a story about America then, told by America now."

With the success of the workshop boosting their confidence, Lin-Manuel and his team turned their focus to casting. It was a given that Lin-Manuel would take on the main role of Hamilton, and many of the other starring parts had already been cast through word of mouth and existing relationships, but they still needed ensemble players and understudies (people who step in when an actor is sick or otherwise unavailable). The casting call in summer 2014 simply asked for actors eighteen and over, of "all ethnicities."

Because interest in the show was so high, the producers tried to keep aspects of it secret while all parts of the production were pieced together. The performers had to wait for the Public Theater to be available but were able to work on the show in a rehearsal space across the street.

What Goes into Making a Show?

sides the writers and directors, there are
ny moving parts and important players in a
sical. All have to work at the same time, and
amlessly, to put together a show.

t Design: The staging,
ckdrops, and props that
lp set each scene. A
rticular challenge to
e set designer David
rins was that the show
d so many rapidly
anging scenes that there
sn't much time to change
e sets between them.

Orchestration: Alex
Lacamoire arranged the
music and conducted a 10-
member orchestra to play
the music of *Hamilton*.

oreography: Creating a
quence of movements for
e actors onstage and
aching each person the
nce, ensuring their precise
vements are in sync with
e other performers. Andy
ankenbuehler was the
oreographer for *Hamilton*,
he was for *In the Heights*
d *Bring It On*.

Costumes: Paul Tazewell had to create costumes that reflected the era while not stifling the actors, who needed to be able to move around a lot

Lighting: Managing the lights is planned as carefully as the other elements of a play, but with less attention from audiences—for example, when to use spotlights to draw attention to a particular character, or when to dim or brighten the lights to set the mood. Howell Binkley was the lighting director for *Hamilton* and won a Tony for his work.

Publicity: *Hamilton*'s hype was already growing but producer Jeffrey Seller and the theater's artistic director Oskar Eustis continued to fan the flames that made *Hamilton* a phenomenon. They handled talking to the media about the show and promoting it to the outside world, while the creators focused on the show.

On an average day of rehearsals, Lin-Manuel would need to talk about music, rewrite lyrics, check in with Ron about historical accuracies, practice his own songs and movements, and even discuss the story structure with Tommy. The full range of responsibilities meant working around the clock, barely eating or sleeping. There's a reason so few people compose *and* star in a musical! Meanwhile, the Public Theater had added a second month to the run, then a third, as tickets had sold out before the show even premiered. Demand was so high that one cast member had to change her name on Facebook to avoid ticket seekers!

If there was a silver lining to being so busy, it was that Lin-Manuel didn't have time to worry or panic about the show's looming start date. There was too much to do.

⋸ LOOK AT MY SON ⋸

In November 2014, Lin-Manuel and Vanessa had their
first son. They named him Sebastian—in part for the
cartoon crab from Disney's *The Little Mermaid* that
Lin-Manuel had loved so much as a child. Lin-Manuel
was in the thick of preparing *Hamilton* for its off-
Broadway debut, but now there was something else in
his life that he felt just as passionate about.

"Dear Theodosia," one of the most moving songs
in the musical, is a duet, featuring Hamilton singing a
lullaby to his baby son Phillip, and Burr singing to his
baby girl, Theodosia. People assumed that Sebastian
Miranda inspired his father to write the lyrics.

"I'll make the world safe and sound for y
—"Dear Theodosia"

Though the lyrics perfectly capture a new father's
mood, Lin-Manuel had written it before Sebastian was
born. However, he said, he could now sing it onstage
with a lot more feeling.

HAMILTON: AN AMERICAN PHENOMENON

Hamilton: An American Musical finally opened for off-Broadway previews on January 20, 2015. Anticipation was high, but nobody—not even Lin-Manuel—could have guessed the phenomenon it would become. It set itself apart from other shows with its content and cast, but also with its high energy—almost nonstop music from beginning to end, with most of the cast onstage for much of the show.

After playing to packed houses for three months, the show closed in the Public Theater. It would reopen for its official Broadway debut at the Richard Rodgers Theatre later that year in August. The producers were eager to go straight to Broadway while interest was still high, but they didn't need to worry; instead of cooling off, the show just got hotter. By the time the show officially opened on August 6, 2015, most weekend performances were sold out for a year in advance, and a wave of newspaper and magazine articles highlighted the upcoming play as one not to miss. It promised to be, one *New York Times* reporter wrote, more than a hit, but a turning point for Broadway.

⇌ THE PERFECT TIME ⇌

In between *Hamilton*'s off-Broadway run and Broadway debut, New York billionaire Donald Trump announced that he was running for president. He ran on an anti-immigration platform that deeply divided America. He often focused on Latino immigrants, describing them as criminals and rallying his supporters with the phrase "Build the wall!" The slogan was a call for a fence along the southern border of the United States to prevent unauthorized immigration from Mexico and South and Central America, though many people felt it represented hostility to immigrants from anywhere.

The moment was right for a story that took a positive view of an immigrant's story, and so *Hamilton* touched a cultural nerve. By portraying people of color as America's founders, it made this story their story, too. By reminding people that an immigrant was among the country's most significant founders, it invited compassion and empathy. By bringing modern music into the historic tale, it made the American origin story feel fresh and vital. *Hamilton* had the effect of showing people a way forward by looking backward. Though it would have been a hit at any time, the moment was perfect for a show like it to appear.

The Other Stars of *Hamilton*

ile Lin-Manuel was clearly the center of all the
tention, *Hamilton* was not a one-star show. It
lped launch and accelerate the careers of several
her brilliant performers.

**lie Odom Jr. (Aaron
r)** is the biggest star
emerge after Lin-Manuel
self. Indeed, it was
lie who won the Tony
rd for Best Actor in a
ical for his performance
Hamilton's rival. He has
e on to appear in the
ie *Harriet* and release an
um of original music, *Mr.*

**Phillipa Soo (Eliza
Schuyler)** left *Hamilton* to
star in her own show, an
adaptation of the beloved
French film *Amélie*. She
has since taken roles on
several television series.

eed Diggs (Thomas Jefferson and Marquis de
`ayette)** had a background in rap music, not
)adway, but in taking on the dual role, he found
 fans and new talents.

Christopher Jackson (George Washington) had already taken the lead in the most successful Broadway show of all time, *The Lion King*, but continued to shine in *Hamilton*.

Jonathan Groff (King George) had major parts in hit TV shows and movies, like *Glee* and *Frozen*, but his performance as King George sealed his place as a Broadway star. Though not a part of the cast at the Public Theater, he joined for the debut on Broadway.

Renée Elise Goldsberry (Angelica Schuyler Church) had appeared in *Rent* and *The Lion King*. She won several awards for her performance in *Hamilton*, including a Tony for Best Actress.

Javier Muñoz (Alexander Hamilton) replaced Lin-Manuel as Hamilton. He had previously taken over the role of Usnavi in *In the Heights*.

The "Comeback" Star

The musical also created a resurgence of interest in the forgotten historical figure at its center, Alexander Hamilton himself. Chernow's book returned to the bestseller list, 11 years after it was originally published, and other publishers quickly put out or reprinted other books about Hamilton. New documentaries about the Treasury secretary ran on PBS and the History Channel. And tourists started visiting Hamilton memorials in big numbers, such as a statue in front of the US Treasury Building in Washington, DC, and Hamilton's grave at the Trinity Church cemetery in Manhattan.

Hamilton even literally "saved face" on the $10 bill. The bill had been slated for redesign and was due to feature Harriet Tubman in place of the founding father, but Hamilton fans came to the rescue, petitioning to save the $10 and instead put Tubman on the $20, replacing Andrew Jackson, the seventh president.

⋛ TICKETS FOR ALL! ⋚

An irony of the show was that while it celebrated immigrants and gave opportunities to performers of color, the price and scarcity of tickets made it inaccessible to the people Lin-Manuel most wanted to reach.

Tickets to *Hamilton* were expensive, as they usually are for Broadway shows. The cheapest tickets cost about two hundred dollars and were the hardest to get, because they were all most people could afford. Prime seats cost over two thousand dollars and sometimes resold for two or three times that amount. Lines were so long to get tickets that many people without free time couldn't even try. Some hired "line sitters"—people who were paid to wait in line for tickets.

The producers and cast wanted the show to be available to everyone, so they introduced a Ham4Ham lottery. Fans could wait outside for the chance to win ten-dollar tickets, and those ticket holders got to sit in the front row. About twenty seats for each

performance were sold
through this lottery system.
Jeffrey Seller had introduced the idea
twenty years earlier with *Rent*. He wanted shows to be
available to the people they were about.

Because people would wait a long time for the lottery
tickets, Lin-Manuel and the rest of the cast started to
perform musical numbers from the show on the street to
reward them for their time. The streetside performances
became a big hit in their own right, often recorded and
shared on social media. While it served the fans of the
show, the #Ham4Ham performances also fed the mania,
inspiring even more people to show up in droves for the
chance at cheap tickets and the opportunity to see the
musical's stars up close. Lin-Manuel collected his favorite
fan videos and made them available on his website.

Eventually, ticket sales and even the Ham4Ham
lottery moved online, so people
could get tickets even if they
couldn't spend hours in line,
hire a line sitter, or take a
day off from work in the
hopes of winning a ten-
dollar ticket.

Lin-Manuel also wanted tickets to be available to students and introduced EduHam, which gives schools material for students so that they can learn about the real people and stories behind the show. The program ends with a free performance. Lin-Manuel credits his parents for EduHam: all the childhood volunteering, meetings, and door-knocking had inspired him. He wanted to share his success and make the show accessible to everyone. The program was initially only available to New York–area schools, but it spread around the country after the show went on tour.

[The student matinees] are the highlights of my life. I can't even begin to describe how it feels.

A REGULAR GUY

As Lin-Manuel's show grew into a worldwide success, he became one of the most famous people in America. Yet he still remained easygoing and approachable, particularly toward his fans. A lot of people wanted to know: How could anyone reach such levels of success while seeming like such a regular guy?

Lin-Manuel explained in more than one interview that by the time *Hamilton* made it big, he already knew who he was. He was married and had a baby. He had a circle of friends who kept him centered. Also, he often explained with a laugh, in his head he had been famous since sixth grade, when he played Conrad Birdie, so nothing had really changed.

> "I knew who I was, and I had friends around me who know who I am."
> —Lin-Manuel Miranda

His busy schedule meant he had to learn to say no, though, which was difficult after so many years of jumping at every chance for a role or job. He decided he didn't really need to be in a commercial aired during the Super Bowl, even if he'd be given a free car. He declined other chances to be on TV or appear at events, too. With up to eight performances of *Hamilton* each week, he didn't have time for much else. He had to look after himself and his health, and carve out time for his wife and baby.

But some opportunities were too exciting to pass up, even a dream come true—like writing the music for a new Disney movie, starring in another, and hosting *Saturday Night Live*. He also made one commercial, for a credit card, because it was made in Washington Heights and celebrated the neighborhood he so loved. But while choosing his projects and juggling his time, Lin-Manuel was discovering that being famous was in and of itself a full-time job.

CHAPTER 6

IN THE EYE OF A HURRICANE

On March 14, 2016, Lin-Manuel returned to the White House by special invitation, this time with the full cast of *Hamilton*. They performed for an audience including area schoolchildren. The Obamas had become friends with Lin-Manuel since his 2009 show. In 2012, Lin-Manuel was part of a fundraiser for President Obama's reelection campaign, and in the time since, they had seen *Hamilton* on Broadway more than once.

Both Barack and Michelle gave speeches before the show began. The president remembered laughing when, seven years before, Lin-Manuel had described Hamilton as a man who "embodies hip-hop."

"And who's laughing now?" the president asked with a big smile, acknowledging that this return trip to the White House was quite a victory lap for Lin-Manuel. He had turned a room full of skeptics into believers in 2009, but nobody could have guessed the success *Hamilton* would become.

"In the character of Hamilton—
a striving immigrant who escaped
poverty, made his way to the New
World, climbed to the top by sheer
force of will and pluck and
determination—Lin-Manuel saw
something of his own family, and
every immigrant family."
—Barack Obama

Michelle simply described it as "the best piece of art in any form I have ever seen."

That day, the cast performed the show without the usual staging and costumes, but still electrified the room. The highlight of the event, though, was a freestyle rap by Lin-Manuel and the president in the Rose Garden. Lin-Manuel was able to draw from his Freestyle Love Supreme experience to make up rhymes on the spot as Barack held up cards with terms like "Oval Office," "Congress," and "Constitution," which Lin-Manuel deftly turned into a rhyme. The performance was streamed live on the White House website.

≡ A SOLEMN MOMENT OF CELEBRATION ≡

A few months later was another important date for Lin-Manuel and the *Hamilton* cast. June 12, 2016, was the night of the Tony Awards. The show was nominated for—and expected to win—a record number of awards, including the coveted prize for Best Musical. But Lin-Manuel was shaken that day by news of a mass shooting targeting Latino and LGBTQ+ people in Orlando, Florida, that had taken place overnight. It was one of the worst in US history, with fifty fatalities and many more people injured. Suddenly, what was supposed to have been a happy day was chilling.

Nobody was surprised when Lin-Manuel was announced as the winner of the Best Original Score for *Hamilton* later that night. He spoke somberly and said he had written not a speech but a poem. He read the sonnet as a tribute to his wife and family, and the victims of the shooting. He teared up as he spoke, finishing with a hush.

Love is love is love is love is love is love is love is love cannot be killed or swept aside.

In the following weeks, he and Jennifer Lopez wrote and recorded a single called "Love Make the World Go Round," with the proceeds going to the families of victims of the shooting. Like Lin-Manuel, the superstar singer and actress is a New Yorker with parents from Puerto Rico. The two recorded the video for the song on top of the Richard Rodgers Theatre, keeping with the tradition of bands like the Beatles and U2 recording videos of surprise rooftop performances.

Lin-Manuel spoke out more and more about his beliefs following the tragedy, particularly defending immigrants and opposing gun violence. As his fame rose, many people asked if he was interested in running for office himself, especially since he was from a political family. Lin-Manuel would shake his head every time. "Please let me write songs," he would say.

If telling the truth is an inherently political act, so be it.

Lin-Manuel Miranda's Awards for *Hamilton*

Lin-Manuel Miranda had already won Tony Awards and been a finalist for a Pulitzer for *In the Heights*. With *Hamilton*, he won too many awards to list, but these are some of the highlights:

Pulitzer Prize for Drama

Tony Awards for Best Book and Best Musical for Lin-Manuel, among 11 Tonys won by the show

Laurence Olivier Award for Outstanding Achievement in Music

Drama Desk Awards for Outstanding Lyrics, Outstanding Music, and Outstanding Book

Latin Recording Academy's President's Merit Award for outstanding contributions to the Latino community

MacArthur Fellowship, or "Genius Grant," given to American artists for "extraordinary originality and dedication"

Grammy Award for Best Musical Theater Album

⋛ LIFE AFTER *HAMILTON* ⋛

In the first year of *Hamilton* on Broadway, Lin-Manuel missed only a single performance. He had a high fever and still tried to get up and go, but Vanessa stopped him. He was replaced for the night by his understudy, Javier Muñoz. He found out later that Jay-Z and Beyoncé had attended *Hamilton* that night. Of course, every night had a few famous faces in the audience, but Lin-Manuel was disappointed to miss the biggest couple in pop music. Maybe that's why he never missed another show.

But eight performances a week is grueling, and shows usually rotate the cast after a year to give the old cast a break, and opportunities to new actors and singers. And so as the musical ended its first year in July 2016, Lin-Manuel stepped down from playing Hamilton, and Javier took up the role full-time. As the show continued to thrive, performances were also planned in cities around the country, including San Francisco, Seattle, and Chicago. Wherever *Hamilton* went, performances sold out as quickly as they had in New York.

But Lin-Manuel didn't have much of a break before he got busy again. Soon after leaving *Hamilton*, he appeared as the host on *Saturday Night Live*. Hosting the comedy variety show was a sign of his new celebrity status, though he joked "most of you at home have no idea who I am." He talked about watching *SNL* as a kid and dreaming of one day hosting it, and then launched into a spoof of "My Shot," with new lyrics about the show.

In one of the best skits that night, Lin-Manuel played an optimistic substitute teacher trying to "reach" a room full of tough-nosed kids through hip-hop, poking fun at himself as a former substitute teacher.

≡ ANOTHER ISLAND STORY ≡

In his spare time, Lin-Manuel had also been writing songs for the new Disney movie *Moana*, a story based on the music and legends of Pacific Islanders and their traditions.

WHAT'S THE STORY?

Moana

Directors: Ron Clements and John Musker

Lyricists: Lin-Manuel Miranda and Opetaia Foa'

Composer: Mark Mancina

Premiere: 2016

Moana is the daughter of the king and queen of the island of Motunui in the Pacific Islands. She accepts her role as the next leader of the island but struggles with the urge to set sail and have adventures on the sea. Her father refuses to let anyone sail beyond the reef due to fear of the ocean. But when the island is struck by a curse that drives away the fish in the reef, Moana must set out to save the island by searching the seas for a mythic demigod named Maui.

The movie was released in November 2016 and was an instant hit with audiences and critics. Moana was a new kind of Disney princess, who fought her own battles and had no love interest. Disney had also made a sincere commitment to including Pacific Islanders in the cast and musicians. But on top of those modern touches, it was a great story with lots of humor and outstanding tunes. The directors had made Lin-Manuel's favorite movie as a boy, *The Little Mermaid*, so it was a dream come true for him to work on it.

Among the best-known songs are "You're Welcome," sung by Dwayne Johnson; "Shiny," sung by Jemaine Clement; and "How Far I'll Go," sung by the movie's rising star, Auli'i Cravalho, all of which were written by Lin-Manuel. He also provided the voice for an unnamed ancestor of Moana singing the song "We Know the Way." With the success of the movie, Lin-Manuel proved he could write infectious Disney hits as capably as he could write hip-hop-influenced Broadway shows. But for him the pleasure came in crafting the songs around Pacific musical traditions and working with the Samoan musician Opetaia Foa'i. Lin-Manuel spent some time in New Zealand, immersing himself in traditional music, before he began to write the soundtrack.

⋛ A NIGHT AT THE OSCARS ⋛

As a child, Lin-Manuel had promised his mother she would be his date if he ever attended the Oscars. When "How Far I'll Go" was nominated for Best Original Song in 2017, he made good on that promise.

People in the entertainment business refer to the EGOT, the rare accomplishment of winning one of each major award in entertainment—Emmy, Grammy, Oscar, and Tony. There is also a PEGOT, for those who have also won the Pulitzer Prize in Drama. By the time Lin-Manuel received his Oscar nomination, he had already won the other four awards.

The "Grand Slam" of Theater

☑ **Pulitzer (literature)**—*Hamilton* won in the Drama category.

☑ **Emmy (television)**—"Bigger!" (from the Tony Awards) won Outstanding Original Music and Lyrics.

☑ **Grammy (music)**—*In the Heights* and *Hamilton* each won Best Musical Theater Album.

☐ **Oscar (movies)**—"How Far I'll Go" was nominated for Best Original Song.

☑ **Tony (Broadway)**—*Hamilton* and *In the Heights* each won Best Original Score.

Unfortunately, Lin-Manuel didn't receive the Oscar that night; it went to Justin Hurwitz, Benj Pasek, and Justin Paul, the songwriting team behind "City of Stars" from the film *La La Land*. But Lin-Manuel was of course flattered to be nominated and thrilled to bring his mother to the Oscars.

⋛ A LATINO SUPERHERO ⋚

Lin-Manuel's career took another unexpected turn
in the summer of 2017 when a TV writer named
Francisco Angones sent him a request. He was one of
the lead writers for a reboot of the Disney animated
series *DuckTales*. The original series ran in the late
1980s and was a mash-up of classic Disney characters
with Indiana Jones–style action-adventure. Francisco,
a Cuban American, wanted to re-create the superhero
character Gizmoduck as Latino. There had been no
Latino superhero characters for him when he was a kid,
and he wanted to fix that in the new series.

Francisco had written the character with Lin-Manuel
in mind, though he felt there was probably no chance
the Broadway star would say yes. To his surprise,
though, Lin-Manuel leaped at the opportunity. He
had loved *DuckTales* as a kid and shared Francisco's
experience of growing up with few Latino role models
to root for on children's cartoon shows. He wanted
to use his fame the best way he knew how, and give
kids of color a chance to see themselves in movies, on
television, and on Broadway.

So Lin-Manuel became the voice of Fenton

Crackshell-Cabrera, a scientific intern who becomes the superhero Gizmoduck when he puts on his metal suit.

⋛ TRAGEDY IN PUERTO RICO ⋛

Sadly, in September 2017, Lin-Manuel had to use his fame for a more serious purpose, when the devastating Hurricane Maria ripped through the Caribbean, doing a lot of damage in Dominica, the US Virgin Islands, and Puerto Rico. The storm also affected Nevis, the birthplace of Alexander Hamilton.

Puerto Rico was already struggling with debt and poverty, and the hurricane added to the misery, destroying thousands of homes and knocking out electricity across the island. The power grid in Puerto Rico was already weakened by Hurricane Danny, which had lashed the island two years earlier, and much of the infrastructure was old and in bad shape. The United States sent emergency supplies to the first islands affected by the storm, so resources were low by the time Puerto Rico needed them.

Lin-Manuel considered Puerto Rico a second home, since he spent so much time there as a child and because his parents were born there. Remembering and honoring where you come from is a theme of his life and his work. So now he felt a call to action. What was the use of having influence if he didn't do anything in times of crisis?

He donated millions of dollars of his own money to charities that were helping the island recover. He also used his fame to correct lies and misinformation and call out politicians who were stalling at sending more resources to Puerto Rico, especially when they described it as "foreign aid." A lot of people seemed to forget that Puerto Rico was part of the United States.

As soon as it was safe to do so, Lin-Manuel traveled to Puerto Rico and personally handed out food, water, and supplies to the people affected by Hurricane Maria. He shared photos and videos with his followers to help raise awareness of the dire situation and encouraged people to donate money.

He also released another single, "Almost Like Praying," a song with lyrics in English and Spanish. It features a section from the song "Maria" from *West Side Story*, a favorite in Puerto Rico. Singers on the track included a number of Puerto Rican and Latin American pop music stars like Gloria Estefan, Jennifer Lopez, and Marc Anthony. Through his many efforts, Lin-Manuel helped raise millions of dollars.

⇌ HAMILTON REMIXED ⇌

In December 2016, Lin-Manuel released *The Hamilton Mixtape*, an album with new versions and remixes of the original cast album along with songs that didn't make it into the show. The performers were a mix of superstars across multiple genres, including Weird Al Yankovic, Kelly Clarkson, the Roots, and John Legend. The highly anticipated album debuted at number one on the Billboard charts, which is rare for compilation albums.

Lin-Manuel thought it would be the first of two or three such albums but ultimately released what would have been the second album one track at a time for free online, as "Hamildrops" in 2018. There wasn't quite enough material for another full album, and he liked the idea of giving his fans something for free. A new song was made available every month throughout the year, performed by artists like Sara Bareilles, the Regrettes, and even Barack Obama, whose farewell speech as president is woven into a remix of "One Last Time."

CHAPTER 7

A MILLION THINGS I HAVEN'T DONE

In February 2018, Lin-Manuel and Vanessa welcomed their second child, Francisco, into the world. Lin-Manuel took some time off from being in the public eye to spend time with his family, though he shared occasional glimpses into their world through social media.

⋛ WE'LL SURELY JOIN THE FIGHT ⋚

The year was already off to a busy start for Lin-Manuel, but he didn't have time to stop. On March 24, Lin-Manuel joined the March for Our Lives in Washington, DC, a demonstration against gun violence. The event culminated in a series of speeches and performances, and Lin-Manuel sang a duet with fellow Broadway star Ben Platt in a mash-up of songs from *Hamilton* and Platt's hit *Dear Evan Hansen*. The lyrics took on new meaning in the context of the march.

$\leqq$ REBOOTING A CLASSIC $\leqq$

Lin-Manuel's next movie, *Mary Poppins Returns*, was
filmed that summer and released in December 2018.
It was his first starring role in a major motion picture. He
had watched the original 1964 movie many times as a
child and was excited to take part in a reboot of the story.

WHAT'S THE STORY?

<u>Mary Poppins Returns</u>

Director: Rob Marshall
Writer: David Magee
Composer and lyricist: Marc Shaiman
Premiere: 2018

Mary Poppins Returns is a sequel to the
classic *Mary Poppins* (1964), starring Emily
Blunt in the title role. The story takes
place 25 years after the original movie.
Michael is grown up, and Mary returns to
serve as a nanny to his three children. She
and Jack the lamplighter whisk the children
away on magical adventures while helping
Michael and Jane save their family home.

His role as Jack the lamplighter is clearly based on Dick Van Dyke's chimney sweep character in the original movie. It includes what Lin-Manuel describes as the toughest ten seconds of his career: he had to light a lamp while riding a bike, steal an apple from a cart, and toss it to a child, all while singing with a British accent.

The movie did well at the box office, and the *New York Times* reviewer remarked that the movie came to life from the moment Lin-Manuel's character appeared on-screen.

G'MORNING AND G'NIGHT, EVERYBODY

With all his projects and appearances, Lin-Manuel's
online followers continued to grow in number. He
became known for sharing greetings every morning
and evening with messages of encouragement and
affirmation on his Twitter profile. Some of these
were collected in a book in 2018, entitled *G'morning,
G'night! Little Pep Talks for Me & You*. He rewrote
the book in Spanish and published it as *¡Buen día,
buenas noches!*, and he recorded an audiobook version
in English.

A TRIP BACK TO WASHINGTON

To round off the year, in December 2018, Lin-Manuel
returned to Washington, DC, this time to receive a
Kennedy Center Honor award along with director
Tommy Kail, musical director Alex Lacamoire, and
choreographer Andy Blankenbuehler for their work
on *Hamilton*. Kennedy Center Honors are for lifetime
achievement in the arts and often come in the twilight
years of a career, but Lin-Manuel and his collaborators
earned it when they were relatively young.

"[T]he creators of *Hamilton* have literally and figuratively changed the face of American culture with daringly original, breathtakingly relevant work."
—Kennedy Center chairman David M. Rubenstein

⋛ BRINGING *HAMILTON* HOME ⋚

Since the early success of *Hamilton*, Lin-Manuel had dreamed of bringing the show to his ancestral home in Puerto Rico. After the hurricanes, he decided that staging the show on the island would be a good way to raise money for the suffering community. While they would make hundreds of low-cost tickets available to residents, there would also be more expensive tickets on offer, with the hopes of attracting wealthy tourists.

Lin-Manuel even gave a million dollars to the University of Puerto Rico in San Juan, the island's capital and biggest city, to renovate and prepare the theater for the show. However, as the entire run quickly sold out, they decided to move the musical to a bigger theater. The performances finally took place in early

2019, and Lin-Manuel returned to the starring role for the first time in almost three years.

Though Lin-Manuel was beloved in Puerto Rico, there had been some debate over the production of the play. Many people in Puerto Rico still felt like a colony and were not eager to watch a musical about the independence of the United States—the country that now colonized them. People wrote angry letters to the editors of local newspapers about the show. They promised to protest when the musical opened.

But in the end, the debut show was peaceful, and the moment Lin-Manuel stepped onto the stage, the entire audience stood and cheered for a full minute, halting the show. It was the biggest ovation Lin-Manuel had ever received. When he sang the song "Hurricane," about a storm that ravaged Nevis when Alexander Hamilton was a child, the audience fell quiet.

I never sang any song with more feeling.

At the end of the show, when Lin-Manuel pulled out a Puerto Rican flag to wave during the curtain call, everybody cheered and many people wept, including Lin-Manuel himself. The show that he had hoped would help heal the island seemed to have done so.

The run of *Hamilton* raised millions of dollars, which Lin-Manuel donted to arts organizations in Puerto Rico, knowing that it would help future artists thrive. He is still very active in Puerto Rico, particularly in raising money for the arts.

⋛ STAR OF THE SCREEN ⋜

Later in 2019, Lin-Manuel played the part of Lee Scoresby in a TV adaptation of the His Dark Materials series by Philip Pullman. His character is a hot-air-ballooning cowboy from Texas. Lin-Manuel said the project was so fun and easy it was practically a vacation from his other work.

He also played a small part in the movie version of *In the Heights*, which was filmed in the summer of 2019 on location in Washington Heights. Now too old to play Usnavi, Lin-Manuel plays Piragua Guy, an unnamed man who sells shaved ice desserts from a colorful cart.

Shooting the movie on location twenty years after he started writing it, and ten years after its Broadway debut, emphasized to Lin-Manuel how much the neighborhood had changed in that time, and also how much the country had changed around it. At the time, writing a story about Latino immigrants chasing their dreams in America was not especially controversial, but now, in the "Build the wall" era, it felt weightier and more important to tell their side of the American story.

> "We're in an age when, for some, considering an immigrant a human being is a radical political act."
> —"The Role of the Artist in the Age of Trump," by Lin-Manuel Miranda (*The Atlantic*, December 2019)

The year 2019 also saw the return of Freestyle Love Supreme, the improv rap show, this time on Broadway, a block from the ongoing performances of

Hamilton. Lin-Manuel was an occasional guest with the cast, as were *Hamilton* stars Daveed Diggs and Christopher Jackson.

As if he didn't have enough on his plate, Lin-Manuel also started composing music for Disney's live-action reboot of the 1989 animated film *The Little Mermaid* with Alan Menken, one of the original composers. The pair of them tweeted teases about working together on the songs, but as yet, none of the soundtrack is available and the movie does not have a release date. Even the cast is unknown, though it is rumored that Daveed Diggs from *Hamilton* will play Lin-Manuel's favorite character, Sebastian the crab.

⋛ CELEBRATING TWO LEGENDS ⋚

Lin-Manuel is also helping to finance and develop a documentary on the legendary Rita Moreno, perhaps the biggest star from Puerto Rico in the twentieth century. She is, Lin-Manuel said, *la reina, punto*. That is: the queen, period. The special will be titled *The Girl Who Decided to Go for It* and will air on public television as part of the *American Masters* series.

Rita Moreno

Rita Moreno was born in Puerto Rico on December 11, 1931, and moved to New York City with her family as a child. She broke into show business as a teenager—appearing in a Broadway show at age 13 and in three movies before she turned 20. Her most famous role is Anita in the 1961 movie version of *West Side Story*. She was the only Puerto Rican cast in the film and won the Oscar for Best Supporting Actress, making her the first Latino person to win an Oscar. She went on to win Tony and Emmy awards, called the "triple crown" of acting. She has also won a Peabody and a Grammy. She was a guest on Lin-Manuel's single "Almost Like Praying," to raise money for Puerto Rico following Hurricane Maria. She will appear in the remake of *West Side Story*, scheduled to premiere in 2020.

At the end of 2019, Lin-Manuel also directed a movie version of Jonathan Larson's *Tick, Tick . . . BOOM!,* the play he had starred in briefly in an off-Broadway reprise in 2014.

VIVO

His biggest upcoming project is *Vivo*, an animated musical about a monkey making the trip from Cuba to Miami to pursue a musical career, which ties the project to his previous works about people from the Caribbean traveling to the mainland to find their fortune. Lin-Manuel is again collaborating with Quiara Alegría Hudes, who wrote the book for *In the Heights*. It is the first movie that is based on his own story and vision, featuring original music and lyrics. In fact, it will be Lin-Manuel's most comprehensive creation since *Hamilton*. Perhaps it will lead to checking off that final box on his PEGOT awards list!

CONCLUSION

HISTORY HAS ITS EYES ON YOU

Broadway shows take several years to write, cast, and rehearse. It's likely that a dozen new musicals in the next few years will have drawn their inspiration from *Hamilton*, and the first of these can already be seen on the stage. One is a reprise of the show *1776*, a musical about American history that originally ran in the late 1960s and early 1970s. It's clear that the producers wanted to capitalize on the interest *Hamilton* generated in musicals about American history.

Perhaps the biggest and most lasting impact of *Hamilton*, though, will be blowing the doors wide open for people of color to audition and play any part. *Hadestown*, which won eight Tony Awards in 2019, featured a diverse cast, where earlier productions of the play had not.

Many other new plays also have writers of color, diverse casts, and stories about the experiences of people of color, such as *Slave Play*, *Marys Seacole*, and *Inheritance*. In its annual list of the most produced plays in the United States in 2019, *Playbill* magazine noted that there were more playwrights of color on the list than ever before. Broadway will never be the same.

The impact spread beyond New York's Theater District, too. In 2017, the British musical *Six* debuted. Written by Toby Marlow and Lucy Moss, it is a historical musical with contemporary music and people of color cast in the roles of white queens—the six wives of Henry VIII. The decision to allow any woman (or nonbinary person) who could sing pop, of any age, body shape, and ethnicity to audition was likely inspired by the fact that it worked so well for Lin-Manuel and *Hamilton*. *Six* is one of the most successful new musicals since *Hamilton*. The show moved to Broadway in February 2020.

⊰ HAMILTON MANIA ⊱

Of course, *Hamilton* itself is still a full-on phenomenon, with plans to resume productions in Los Angeles, New York, and London in 2021. Performances in Australia and France are planned, and a Spanish translation is underway for a production in Mexico City. Back on Broadway, the show is expected to run for years at the Richard Rodgers Theatre. It has already placed among the top-ten most profitable musicals of all time, alongside shows that have run much longer.

Hamilton was filmed onstage with its original cast in 2016 to run in movie theaters in 2021. However, the

Most Successful Broadway Musicals of All Time

1. *The Lion King*
   (1997)—$1.7 billion

2. *Wicked*
   (2003)—$1.4 billion

3. *The Phantom of the Opera*
   (1988)—$1.3 billion

4. *Chicago*
   (1975, revival 1997)—
   $680 million

5. *The Book of Mormon*
   (2011)—$650 million

6. *Hamilton*
   (2015)—$640 million

7. *Mamma Mia!*
   (2001)—$625 million

8. *Jersey Boys*
   (2005)—$560 million

9. *Aladdin*
   (2014)—$460 million

10. *Beauty and the Beast*
    (1994)—$430 million

COVID-19 pandemic in 2020 changed those plans. Instead, it aired on the Disney+ subscription service in the summer of 2020, so people could see the original Broadway version at home.

The *Hamilton* fandom has become an internet subculture, with millions of "Hamilfans" discussing the show, sharing their role-playing costumes (cosplay), and recording their own renditions of the songs. Among the flood of *Hamilton* fan content are #HamilKids and #HamilTots, which show children singing the songs from *Hamilton*, dancing to the album, and dressing up as the show's characters. Lin-Manuel frequently engages with fans through Twitter and Instagram, and will often answer fan questions about the show, share people's *Hamilton*-themed photos and videos, or crack jokes. He's generally up for a selfie, too, if fans spot him out and about in New York.

WHO GETS TO TELL YOUR STORY?

With such success behind him, it can be easy to forget that Lin-Manuel is still young. He could have a dozen more shows in front of him and—like his mentor Stephen Sondheim—revolutionize Broadway more than once. Only time will tell, but even if *Hamilton* is the highlight of his career, his place in history seems assured.

However, one lesson Lin-Manuel got from writing *Hamilton* is that you can't control your legacy. Alexander Hamilton was obsessed with his own reputation but suffered from gossip while alive and malicious lies after he died. He had largely faded into obscurity until Ron Chernow and Lin-Manuel Miranda revived him.

What is a legacy? It's planting seeds in a garden you never get to see.

But his legacy is sure to go down in history books. His talent and willingness to experiment have led many to compare him to William Shakespeare, the famous English playwright, whose work we still read and perform over four hundred years after his death.

"Lin does exactly what Shakespeare does. He takes the language of the people and heightens it. . . . He tells the foundational myths of his country. By doing that, he makes the country the possession of everybody."
—Oskar Eustis

Though his next Broadway show may be years away, Lin-Manuel's fans have plenty to look forward to in the near future, particularly the *In the Heights* movie. And, of course, they can continue to follow Lin-Manuel's fan-friendly social media presence, with his daily affirmations and behind-the-scenes peeks at his works in progress.

His work in Puerto Rico also continues. In January 2020, an earthquake rocked the island, and Lin-Manuel immediately began driving attention to the new tragedy and recommending places to donate money to help.

While he writes and works nonstop, Lin-Manuel's life is still primarily centered around his family: his parents, his sister, and especially Vanessa, Sebastian, and Francisco. Lin-Manuel knows his biggest task ahead is raising his sons and making the world a better place for them.

While not much is known about his next steps, it is likely he will continue to tell stories that celebrate immigrants, empower the poor, and speak truth to power.

Look around, look around at how lucky we are to be alive right now.

<u>Timeline</u>

★

January 16
Lin-Manuel
Miranda is
born in New
York, NY.

★

Lin-Manuel is
accepted at the
highly competitive
Hunter College
Elementary School.

1980

1985

Rent debuts on
Broadway and
becomes one of the
top musicals of
the 1990s.

Lin-Manuel graduates
from Hunter College
High School and
enrolls at Wesleyan
University.

1994

1998

Lin-Manuel sees his first live musical, *Les Misérables*, with his family. It is the most successful musical of the decade.

Billboard introduces charts for rap music.

1987

1989

Lin-Manuel stages a one-act version of *In the Heights* at Wesleyan University.

2000

2005

Lin-Manuel takes Vanessa Nadal to *Wicked* on one of their first dates. It is the top musical of the decade.

In the Heights premieres on Broadway.

Barack Obama is elected president.

2008

Lin-Manuel and Vanessa holiday in Mexico, where Lin-Manuel reads Ron Chernow's biography of Alexander Hamilton and comes up with the idea for Hamilton.

Lin-Manuel and Vanessa's first child, Sebastian, is born.

2013

2014

Bring It On debuts on Broadway, featuring music by Lin-Manuel Miranda.

Lin-Manuel performs
the song "Alexander
Hamilton" at the White
House for the Obamas.

Lin-Manuel
marries
Vanessa Nadal.

2009   2010

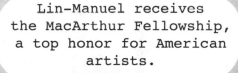

Lin-Manuel receives
the MacArthur Fellowship,
a top honor for American
artists.

2015

Hamilton debuts and
quickly becomes the
hottest musical of
the decade.

The Disney movie *Moana* is released, featuring several songs by Lin-Manuel.

2016

2017

September—October
Puerto Rico is devastated by Hurricane Maria.

2019

Lin-Manuel resumes the role of Alexander Hamilton for the first time in nearly three years in San Juan, Puerto Rico.

Lin-Manuel and
Vanessa's second child,
Francisco, is born.

2018

Mary Poppins Returns
is released,
costarring Lin-Manuel.

The original cast
movie of *Hamilton* is
released.

2020

2021

The film version of
In the Heights is due
for release.

Further Reading

→ *Alexander Hamilton, Revolutionary*
by Martha Brockenbrough
(Feiwel & Friends, 2017)

→ *G'morning, G'night! Little Pep Talks for
Me & You* by Lin-Manuel Miranda
and Jonny Sun (Random House, 2018)

→ *Hamilton: The Revolution* by
Lin-Manuel Miranda and Jeremy McCarter
(Grand Central, 2016)

→ *Where Is Broadway?* by Douglas Yacka and
Francesco Sedita (Penguin Workshop, 2019)

Websites

→ gilderlehrman.org/programs-and-events
/hamilton-education-program

The Hamilton Education Program provides free
lesson plans to schools incorporating *Hamilton*
into history classes, and the opportunity for
students to get free tickets.

→ twitter.com/Lin_Manuel

Lin-Manuel Miranda's personal Twitter feed,
featuring regular insights into his creative
processes and encouraging messages.

Glossary

book: In theater, the spoken (unsung) dialogue in a musical.

Broadway: Relating to theaters of 500 or more seats in the Theater District of New York City.

choreography: The design, planning, and arrangement of the dance and movement in a show.

colonization: The process of a people resettling in a new place where they take over as a cultural and economic power.

critic: In theater, a person who watches and reviews plays with expert analysis for newspaper, TV, or radio.

director: In theater, the supervisor of, and ultimate decision maker on, all aspects of the show, especially casting decisions and coaching of performers.

Glossary

Latino: A person who is from or descended from people from the Spanish- and Portuguese-speaking countries south of the United States.

libretto: The song lyrics in a musical.

lyricist: The person who writes the libretto.

off-Broadway: Relating to theaters of fewer than 500 seats in the Theater District of New York City or (sometimes) outside the district but in or near Manhattan.

ovation: A long round of enthusiastic clapping and cheering, often with the audience standing, at the end of a performance.

people of color: People who are not white or of primarily European heritage.

Glossary

producer: In theater, people responsible for financing and publicizing a show.

Pulitzer Prize: Award given for outstanding achievement in American literature, including drama.

revival (also reprise): In theater, a new production of a play or musical that has already run.

skit: A very short and humorous play.

social justice: Awareness of and interest in fixing inequality in one's culture, particularly related to race, gender, and social class.

Tony Awards: Awards for Broadway shows given every June.

Glossary

understudy: A person prepared to take on a role if the main actor is sick or otherwise unable to perform.

Index

Index

Index

Index

Index

Index

FOLLOW THE TRAIL!

TURN THE PAGE FOR A SNEAK PEEK AT THESE TRAILBLAZERS BIOGRAPHIES!

⋜ LOST IN THE LIBRARY ⋜

Amelia might not have been able to spell beware, but she did very well at school and worked hard in her lessons. The Earhart girls played outdoors whenever they could, but when they did have to stay inside, Amelia liked to read in her grandfather's library. She had to lie on the floor because some of the books were so large and heavy that they were difficult to read any other way, but Amelia didn't care.

Two of Amelia's favorites were *Black Beauty* and *The Tale of Peter Rabbit*, but she also enjoyed books by authors such as Charles Dickens and Alexandre Dumas. These books were filled with adventures in faraway places—adventures like the ones she hoped to have someday.

⋛ NEW JOURNEYS ⋛

Soon, the Earhart sisters would swap their imaginary adventures for real ones. Edwin's job working for railroad companies meant he had to travel a lot. Sometimes his family traveled with him, though often he traveled with Amy or alone, leaving the girls in the care of their grandparents.

In England after her transatlantic flight, Amelia had
bought a small Avro Avian airplane from Lady Mary
Heath, a famous aviatrix. Lady Mary had used the plane
in 1928 to make a record-breaking solo flight, becoming
the first person to fly from Cape Town, South Africa,
to Croydon, England. The journey of more than ten
thousand miles took Lady Mary three and a half months
and included stops in Uganda, Egypt, and Sudan.

Lady Mary Heath

Lady Mary Heath was a record-breaking pilot,
an Olympic athlete, a writer, and a women's
rights activist. In the 1920s, Lady Mary
fought the International Commission for Air
Navigation for women to be allowed to become
commercial pilots—pilots who transport people
or goods on planes. Lady Mary won and became
Great Britain's first female commercial pilot

Amelia shipped the Avro Avian to New York. It
arrived with a note that read:

To Amelia Earhart from Mary Heath,
    Always think with your stick forward.

When up in the air, pilots need to maintain their plane's speed to keep it flying. To do this, pilots fly with the stick (or controls) in a forward position. To Amelia, the message meant that it was time to take to the sky again!

Great Planes: Avro Avian

Seats: 2
Wingspan: 28 ft. (8.5 m)
Manufacturer: Avro, Great Britain
Engine: Cirrus II air-cooled inline engine
Horsepower: 84 hp
Speed: 102 mph (164 kmh)
Max height: 18,000 ft. (5,500 m)
Weight: 1,130 lb. (513 kg)
Date of manufacture: 1927

The derby didn't go without a hitch. Of the nineteen planes that started the race, only eleven finished the course. Some pilots flew off course, some crash-landed during refueling stops, and one woman, Marvel Crosson, died after her parachute failed to open when she bailed out over the mountains. Amelia herself had a lucky escape after her plane flipped over when she came in to land on a refueling stop, damaging the propeller. Thanks to her many years of experience with planes, Amelia was able to make the repairs and get into the sky again quickly enough to finish in third place, behind Louise Thaden in first and Gladys O'Donnell in second.

Despite the dangers, the female pilots had shown the world just how brave and talented women could be. In the process, many had become good friends. A few days after the race, Amelia invited the fliers to a meeting in her hotel room and suggested they set up a club for female pilots.

Early in the civil rights movement, black people made up the majority of Martin's supporters, but by the 1960s, Martin had won over the hearts and minds of many white people as well. Although this was a great success for the movement, those who were against equal rights for black people saw this as problematic. It was not uncommon for Martin to receive hate letters in the mail or threatening phone calls in which people vowed to kill him and his family. Sometimes Martin was even harassed by the police in a city he was visiting.

Police Brutality

For several decades following the abolition of slavery, only white men were allowed to serve on the police force. Many police officers were former Confederate soldiers and members of hat groups that discriminated against black people They often abused their power by threatening, intimidating, and even killing black people. This violence continued throughout the civil rights movement even in the midst of peaceful protests. In modern America, there continue t be reasons for black communities to distrust some police officers, and organizations such Black Lives Matter have formed to seek justic

On October 19, 1960, Martin was among over fifty protesters who took part in a department store sit-in. Located in Atlanta, Rich's department store had a special restaurant and fitting room area called the Magnolia Room. Even though black people could purchase items from Rich's, only white people could sit in the Magnolia Room and try on clothes there. When Martin and the other protesters entered the Magnolia Room and refused to leave, the police arrested them. Eventually everyone was released—except Martin.

Martin was the last leader to speak, and his speech would resonate with listeners all over the globe. It remains one of the most quoted speeches of all time.

After Martin's speech, A. Philip Randolph asked the crowd to take a pledge to commit to the struggle and support the fight against segregation and racism.

I pledge my heart and my mind and my body unequivocally and without regard to personal sacrifice, to the achievement of social peace through social justice.

The crowd responded with a resounding, "I do pledge!"

The March on Washington concluded with one of Martin's first mentors, Morehouse College president Dr. Benjamin E. Mays, giving a blessing. Then, in a beautiful moment of solidarity, the crowd joined together to sing the anthem of the civil rights movement, "We Shall Overcome."

Given the success of the march, President Kennedy scheduled a meeting with the Big Ten and other march leaders immediately afterward. The group met him at the White House, and he congratulated them on the peaceful demonstration. As the march had been so well attended and successful, President Kennedy hoped it would improve the chances that Congress would support his civil rights act.

A NEW PARTNERSHIP

Jay-Z and Beyoncé released a single together, "'03 Bonnie and Clyde." On the track, Jay-Z sings, "All I need in this life of sin is me and my girlfriend," to which Beyoncé replies, "Down to ride till the very end, is me and my boyfriend." For some fans, this was confirmation enough that the two were dating.

But even with rumors swirling, Beyoncé and Jay-Z refused to confirm or deny that they were together. When asked about the nature of their relationship, Jay-Z told one reporter, "She's beautiful. Who wouldn't wish she was their girlfriend? Maybe one day."

Bonnie and Clyde

Jay-Z and Beyoncé's track was named after two infamous criminals who traveled the United States together in the 1930s. Bonnie and Clyde led police on a chase across the country, robbing several businesses and murdering 13 people. The two were finally tracked down by a Texas Ranger in Bienville Parish, Louisiana, where they were shot and killed.

Every part of the performance had to be exactly right, from the backup dancers to the lighting. Her outfit, a tight black bodysuit, took two hundred hours to put together. Due to the intense rehearsal schedule, Beyoncé lost weight, and the waist had to be taken in repeatedly to ensure a flattering fit.

The set began with an explosion of red-and-white flares and a giant white outline of Beyoncé above the stage. Then the singer emerged to perform "Love on Top." Later, Beyoncé was joined by Michelle and Kelly, who rose up through hidden trapdoors to sing a few of Destiny's Child's greatest hits to the 70,000-strong crowd. To wrap up the performance, Beyoncé turned down the tempo and ended on the emotionally charged "Halo."